Unlimited Submission?

How Romans 13:1–5 has been
incorrectly used to silence
Christians and the Church

by Dan Fisher

Black Robe Publishing
1230 N. Sooner Road
Edmond, OK 73034
www.danfisherbrr.com

Printed in the United States of America

ISBN: 978-0-578-23761-9

Contents

"No government is to be submitted to, at the expense of that which is the sole end of all government—the common good and safety of society."
Pastor Jonathan Mayhew, 1749

"A slavish submission to tyranny is a proof of a very sordid and base mind."
Pastor Samuel West, May 29, 1776

"When a constitutional government is converted into tyranny, … there ought not to be the least doubt but that a remedy is provided in the laws of God and reason, for their preservation; nor ought resistance in such case to be called rebellion."
Pastor Elizur Goodrich, 1787

"Is there no case in which a people may resist government? Yes, there is one such case; and that is, when rulers usurp a power oppressive to the people."
Pastor Joseph Lathrop, Dec. 14, 1787

Introduction

"You are a Christian and it is your duty under God to submit to government; no matter what—and you are sinning if you don't!"

"Our Founders and Framers were sinning when they defied England, fought for their independence, and eventually formed what we know today as the United States of America."

"Because Jesus, Paul, and the other Apostles were unengaged in their government and did not call upon their followers to rebel against the tyranny of their day, Christians should stay out of politics and submit to whatever government they find themselves living under—no matter the tyranny."

How often have you heard someone, especially a Christian pastor or Bible teacher, make declarations like these? Are they right?

Like you I suspect, I have grappled most of my life with the question of whether or not the Bible, especially in Romans 13:1–5, teaches *unlimited* submission to governmental author-ity. Today, Christians are told by many leaders in the faith that they owe *unlimited* submission to those in authority and that they are sinning if they do not submit. But does God intend that believers submit to government even when its decrees/

laws mandate such evils as human slavery or the murder of the preborn?

It is imperative that we find a biblically consistent answer to this question. Must we submit to a government that denies or covers up the truth? Must we submit to a government that abuses the innocent or allows them to be abused?

It is my contention that spiritual leaders have been un-intentionally (out of ignorance), or worse yet, intentionally shackling Christians for years with a flawed interpretation of Romans 13:1–5. I believe they have misunderstood this passage generally, and specifically as to how it applies to those living in a republic like ours. Consequently, Christian people who would normally stand against evils like the murder of the preborn have come to believe that they owe *slavish, unlimited* submission to their government and that they would be committing the sin of rebellion if they stood up against a government that promotes/allows such evil. Obeying their spiritual advisors, the American church, for the most part, stands by doing little to stop the wickedness that is allowed to flourish all around them.

Before I am misunderstood, let me state the obvious: submission to *proper* authority, especially that of governing authorities, **is clearly** taught in Scripture:

> "Let every soul be subject to the governing authorities. For there is no authority except from God, and the authorities that exist are appointed by God. Therefore whoever resists the authority resists the ordinance of God, and those who resist will bring judgment on themselves. For rulers

are not a terror to good works, but to evil. Do you want to be unafraid of the authority? Do what is good, and you will have praise from the same. For he is God's minister to you for good. But if you do evil, be afraid; for he does not bear the sword in vain; for he is God's minister, an avenger to execute wrath on him who practices evil. Therefore you must be subject, not only because of wrath but also for conscience' sake."

—Rom. 13:1–5, NKJV

"Remind them to be subject to rulers and authorities, to obey, to be ready for every good work, to speak evil of no one, to be peaceable, gentle, showing all humility to all men."   —Titus 3:1–2, NKJV

"Therefore submit yourselves to every ordinance of man for the Lord's sake, whether to the king as supreme, or to governors, as to those who are sent by him for the punishment of evildoers and for the praise of those who do good. For this is the will of God, that by doing good you may put to silence the ignorance of foolish men –"

—1 Peter 2:13–15, NKJV

"Therefore I exhort first of all that supplications, prayers, intercessions, and giving of thanks be made for all men, for kings and all who are in authority, that we may lead a quiet and peaceable life in all godliness and reverence. For this is good and acceptable in the sight of God our Savior,"

—1 Timothy. 2:1–3, NKJV

Scripture unquestionably teaches that followers of Christ should be known for their respect **for** and submission **to** *proper* authority. But, the unavoidable question is: "Does this include evil authorities as well?" Must we submit to every dictate of authority—especially if in doing so we violate God's laws and principles or are forced to stand by while evil prevails? Believers who take their walk with God seriously must know the answer to this most important question.

Obviously, no one struggles with submission when good people are in authority and are using that authority properly. The problem arises when evil people are in charge and use their authority to tyrannize the people and to perpetuate evil. When this happens does the Bible actually teach that Christians have no other option but to submit and pray? This is the great dilemma we will examine in this book.

For those of us living in America where we have enjoyed more than two centuries of freedom and self-governance, the answer to this dilemma will have drastic and far-reaching consequences for our children, grandchildren, and great grandchildren. The answer may well determine whether we and/or our children will live free or under the heavy hand of tyranny. Do we really want to see the Gospel driven underground in America? If the church continues to disengage, we very well may. For those of us who claim the name of Christ, especially those who hold positions of leadership in the church, the question of *unlimited* submission to government has immediate implications—ones for which we dare not hesitate to find a solid biblical answer.

Chapter 1

Believers Haven't Always Practiced Unlimited Submission to Governmental Authority

Let us begin by examining the question, "Have believers throughout the centuries always submitted to tyrants?" The simple answer is, "No!" Even many of the biblical heroes we celebrate defied their governmental authorities. What's more, these believers actually received God's approval for their defiance. Students of Scripture, and even the casual reader, will be familiar with numerous examples of this.

Heroes in Scripture Who Defied Authority

1. Exodus 1:15–21 tells the story of the courageous Hebrew midwives who defied Pharaoh's command to murder all of the Hebrew boys once they were born. These women risked their own lives in order to save these Jewish babies and in doing so, received God's approval and blessing. Therefore, Christian leaders rightly hold up these believers as heroes of the faith. *(But, according to the "unlimited*

submission" interpretation, the midwives would have been in violation of Romans 13:1–5, as well as other similar passages.)

2. Exodus 2:1–10 tells the similar story of Moses's parents who also defied Pharaoh's command in order to save their baby boy. Just as with the Hebrew midwives, God not only approved of the actions of Moses's parents, but also blessed their plan and sovereignly placed Moses in the house of Pharaoh where he became a member of royalty—even though this was all done in defiance to governmental authority. Hebrews 11:23 actually commends Moses' parents for their defiance. Christian leaders rightly hold up Moses' parents as heroes of the faith. *(But, according to the "unlimited submission" interpretation, Moses' parents would have been in violation of Romans 13:1–5, as well as other similar passages.)*

3. Exodus 2:11–15 and 4:29–14:31 tell the story of how Moses defied Pharaoh in initially leaving Egypt as a fugitive from the law and then returned to free the Israelites from slavery. Throughout that whole story, by obeying God, Moses disobeyed Pharaoh—the lawful governmental authority of Egypt. Hebrews 11:24–29 even commends Moses for his faith to obey God while defying Pharaoh. Again, Christian leaders rightly revere Moses as a major hero of the faith. *(But, according to the "unlimited submission" interpretation, Moses would have been in violation of Romans 13:1–5, as well as other similar passages.)*

4. Esther 4:10–16, 5:1–2 tells the story of the heroine,

Queen Esther, and her courage to approach the king un-invited—even though she risked the penalty of capital punishment for doing so. Of course, she did this in order to save her Jewish people from being annihilated due to the plan of a powerful, yet evil man named Haman. Once again, God honored Esther for her faith and courage as she defied governmental authority to save innocent lives. Yet, Christian leaders rightly celebrate Esther as a heroine of the faith. *(But, according to the "unlimited submission" interpretation, Esther would have been in violation of Romans 13:1–5, as well as other similar passages.)*

5. Daniel 3:1–23 tells the story of the three Hebrew men, Shadrach, Meshach, and Abed-Nego, who defied Nebuchadnezzar, King of Babylon, by refusing to bow down to his image of gold. They were willing to risk the fiery furnace and certain death rather than to disobey the first two of God's Ten Commandments. Again, Christian leaders correctly consider these believers heroes of the faith. *(But, according to the "unlimited submission" interpretation, Shadrach, Meshech, and Abed-Nego would have been in violation of Romans 13:1–5, as well as other similar passages.)*

6. Daniel 6:1–23 tells the story of Daniel the Prophet who defied King Darius by continuing to pray to the God of Israel even though he knew it was illegal. Daniel, like his three Hebrew friends above, was willing to risk the lion's den rather than limit his fellowship with God. And yet

again, Christian leaders rightly honor Daniel as a hero of the faith. *(But, according to the "unlimited submission" interpretation, Daniel would have been in violation of Romans 13:1–5, as well as other similar passages.)*

7. Matthew 12:1–14 and John 18:31 tell of how Jesus defied the lawful Jewish authorities of His day by refusing to obey the Jewish Sabbath laws the rabbis had written to shackle the people. Even though the Jewish authorities ruled by permission of the Roman government, and even though the Rabbis were evil and guilty of twisting and adding to God's commands, they still wielded valid governmental authority. Obviously, Christian leaders boldly worship Jesus as *the* ultimate hero of the faith. *(But, according to the "unlimited submission" interpretation, Jesus would have been in violation of Romans 13:1–5, as well as other similar passages.)*

8. Acts 5:27–29, 12:1–4, and 16:19–24 tell how the Apostles and early Christians defied the Jewish and Roman authorities by refusing to stop preaching the Gospel. Like so many before them, they were willing to risk life and limb to obey God's command. We rightly hold them up as examples for all believers to follow. *(But, according to the "unlimited submission" interpretation, the Apostles and early Christians would have been in violation of Romans 13:1–5, as well as other similar passages.)*

9. Hebrews 11:32–38 tells the story of multitudes of oth-

er believers who defied ungodly governmental authority because obedience to God was more important to them than comfort or life. Christian leaders correctly celebrate these believers as heroes of the faith as well. *(But—this is getting ridiculous—according to the "unlimited submission" interpretation, these many unnamed believers would have been in violation of Romans 13:1–5, as well as other similar passages.)*

What is of special note is that the above heroes are all included in God's eternal "hall of faith"—even though they disobeyed human governmental authorities in the process. Like countless others who also found themselves in the unenviable position of having to choose between obeying earthly or heavenly authority, they made the right decision and chose to honor God rather than men. We correctly celebrate and hold these people up as role models for all to emulate. But, if Paul, by the inspiration of the Holy Spirit, teaches in Romans 13:1–5 that believers must *always* submit to *all* governmental authority, weren't these believers sinning when they defied authority and doesn't this create a major contradiction in Scripture?

Ironically, many preachers and politicians who believe Romans 13:1–5 requires *unlimited* submission to governmental authority seem content with operating in a world of spiritual dissonance, robustly applauding the above-mentioned examples of defiance while decrying any modern defiance of authority. How can they justify this apparent contradiction? Either men like Daniel and the Apostles were heroes of the faith, understanding that there are times when rebellion is

13

the only godly response to tyranny, or they were sinful rebels who were disobeying God by refusing to submit to the evil authorities under whose heavy hand they lived.

Worse yet, if the "unlimited submission" interpretation is correct, then a much larger problem looms—Jesus was wrong when He refused to submit to numerous Jewish laws in His day. We must remember that under Roman rule, the Jewish authorities had the power to make and enforce many of their religious traditions into law—thus making their laws just as official as those of the Romans. Jesus, of course, rebuked them for their unbiblical traditions (sometimes enacted into law) telling the Rabbis they had made "the word of God of no effect" by their traditions (Mark 7:13). Accordingly, He ignored their unjust laws. Yet, even as misguided and wrong as they were, those Jewish leaders were "official" government authorities wielding government-sanctioned power. So, if God truly demands *unlimited* submission to all governmental authority, didn't Jesus sin when He disobeyed the Jewish authorities? Wasn't He in violation of the very principle of *unlimited submission* He would later inspire the Apostle Paul to impose upon every believer in Romans 13:1–5?

Of course, this **cannot** be since Scripture clearly declares Jesus to be the sinless Son of God. If He had sinned even once, we are hopelessly lost without a Savior. Since this is obviously not the case, there must be a reasonable solution to this *apparent* contradiction. The solution is actually quite simple: Jesus, who was divine and without sin and who knew the hearts of all men, disregarded the frivolous traditions and laws of the Rabbis knowing that their misuse of power rendered them illegitimate rulers, void of *true*, "God-ordained" governmental authority. Jesus clearly demonstrated the principle that godly people have no obligation to submit to tyrannous authorities and their godless decrees.

Extrabiblical Heroes Who Defied Authority

It is not just heroes of Scripture we applaud for defying tyranny. History is filled with stories of courageous individuals whose actions we equally celebrate today who defied the tyrants of their day. Like the heroes of Scripture, we hold these brave individuals up as worthy role models. Consider these examples:

1. We admire and honor our American Founders and Framers for defying the tyranny of England to secure the liberties we all enjoy today. Millions of Americans celebrate their commitment and courage every Thanksgiving and Fourth of July.

2. We bestow hero status on abolitionists like Harriet Tubman and Harriet Beecher Stowe for seeing slavery as the unconscionable evil it is and for taking action and defying the authorities to help runaway slaves find freedom.

3. We retell the stories of Corrie Ten Boom, Oskar Schindler, and Dietrich Bonhoeffer who defied the German authorities to save hundreds of Jews and other political dissidents from the evil clutches of the Nazis in mid-twentieth century Germany.

4. We revere heroes like Martin Luther King, Jr. for stand-
    ing against unjust governmental norms and the Jim
    Crow laws of the 1950s and '60s. Every third Monday in
    January we celebrate a national holiday to honor their
    fight for racial equality.

But, based upon the popular "unlimited submission" interpretation of Romans 13:1–5, shouldn't we be denouncing these
people as rebels and anarchists for their defiance to authority?
Ironically, as in the case of the Bible heroes listed earlier, the
very spiritual and political leaders who denounce defiance to
modern tyranny enthusiastically applaud the above examples.
Even though these leaders deplore evils like abortion, they are
so strongly committed to the *unlimited submission* position that
they not only submit to evil laws/decrees but also condemn
anyone who would even suggest defiance to them. Their solution: patiently and prayerfully wait until the "political stars"
perfectly align and the governmental authorities, specifically
the U.S. Supreme Court, reverse themselves and end such
injustices.

What Modern Preachers Say

Sadly, most modern preachers/teachers seem bent on a faulty
understanding of Romans 13:1–5 specifically and of the totality
of Scripture generally. In the attempt to build large churches
and secure the applause and approval of men, they have wa-
tered down and censored their message until they have suc-
cessfully neutered the Christian Church in America. Unwilling

to take a difficult stand for righteousness, they have acquiesced to the evil of our day and use their flawed interpretation of Scripture, mainly of Romans 13:1–5, to justify their compromise. Even worse, they have taught their congregations to do the same. Employing their unbiblical *unlimited* submission interpretation of Romans 13:1–5, they ignore the many stories in Scripture of godly men and women who defied the tyrants of their day and teach that God demands *total* submission to *all* in authority—when God actually calls upon believers to stand for righteousness; even if that stand requires disobedience and defiance to earthly authorities and magistrates.

Of course, in order to appease guilty consciences, modern preachers offer a few exceptions and "allow" defiance in examples of "extreme" tyranny (as if *all* tyranny isn't extreme). One such "exception" or "concession" they are willing to make is when authorities forbid believers to "preach the Gospel." In this instance, they are quick to boldly declare that we must preach the Gospel whether it is legal to do so or not! But, this concession is really nothing more than a smoke screen employed to sidestep the real issue. Clearly, believers must boldly preach and share the Gospel even when they are forbidden to do so by their magistrates. But, that is not the real question—every believer agrees with this. The real question is: "Is this the only time when defiance to authority is acceptable?" Actually, there are many examples in Scripture (and outside of Scripture) of believers defying authority (for which they received God's commendation), not because they were being forbidden to "preach the truth," but because they felt compelled to stand against tyranny. The defiance of the Hebrew midwives had nothing to do with "preaching the Gospel." Queen Esther was not being forbidden to practice her faith but was, in fact, interposing herself to save her people. Corrie Ten Boom and Dietrich Bonheoffer's defiance had nothing to do with being forbidden to preach the Gospel.

One has to wonder just how sincere these modern spiritual leaders really are since they refuse to preach the "whole Gospel" now when it is legal to do so! So, what would lead us to believe they would have the courage to preach the whole Gospel if it was actually against the law to do so?

One other concession for defiance these modern "limited submission" preachers/teachers are willing to make is in the case of the government's laws/policies forcing believers to sin personally. Even though this certainly is a case for defiance, again, this is another example of teaching/preaching half-truths. Just as in the previous concession, there are many examples, both in the Bible and in secular history, when godly men and women defied authorities for reasons other than because they were being forced to sin personally. Again, Queen Esther was not being forced to sin when she defied the law but did so in the attempt to thwart the plan of an evil man who wanted to slaughter her people. Paul and the other apostles did not defy their governmental authorities because they were being forced to sin personally but because they were attempting to obediently carry out God's mission to preach the Gospel and plant churches all over the world. Corrie Ten Boom and Dietrich Bonheoffer were not defying their government because they were being forced to sin personally but acted in defiance because they were attempting to save innocent people from the evil Nazis. The same could be said for Martin Luther King, Jr. and multiplied thousands of others who defied history's tyrants.

Certainly, every believer should agree that defiance to authority is biblically warranted when it is illegal to preach the Gospel or when we are being forced to sin personally, but these are only two of the MANY examples of when defiance is the godly response. Any time evil is perpetrated by or allowed by authorities, that is the time for righteous defiance. My good friend, Pastor Matt Trewhella, says it like this, "When the state commands that which God forbids or when the state forbids that which God commands, we must disobey." Brother Matt is right! Insisting on only these two concessions is a thinly veiled cop-out by those who believe in the "unlimited submission" interpretation of Romans 13:1–5. Sadly, most Christians today see these concessions as the only biblical reasons for resisting tyranny and seem perfectly content to offer *unlimited* submission to illegitimate magistrates; while offering little or no objection to the evil taking place all around them. Of course, to save face, Christian leaders hold countless rallies decrying evils like abortion, but little of any real substance is ever actually done to stop the holocaust. Christians help pass endless regulations aimed at reducing evil, but these impotent measures have no real impact on lessening the injustice in our land. Consequently, the overall message conveyed to most believers today is one of pacifism and capitulation. Christians are basically told to wait, pray, and hope for a benevolent government to do the right thing—all while evils like the murder of millions of innocent preborn babies are perpetrated across all fifty states. Surely this cannot be what God is saying in Romans 13:1–5.

The truth is the Bible does not teach *unlimited* submission to governmental authority. As we will see, God's definition of a proper government, one that deserves the submission of believers, is a very narrow one.

Questions to ponder for those who either preach/teach or accept the unlimited submission message today:

> Had you been living in nineteenth century America, would you have said it was a sin to help slaves escape to freedom based upon the U.S. Supreme Court's 1857 *Dred Scott v. Sandford* decision that said that Blacks were mere property and could be owned and sold like chattel? Would you have instructed fellow believers to patiently wait and pray for the Supreme Court to reverse itself— while leaving millions of their fellow brothers and sisters in slavery?

> Had you been living in the 1920s and '30s, would you have told fellow believers to stand down and simply pray while certain Americans deemed unfit to reproduce were forcibly sterilized simply because the Supreme Court said that practice was constitutional in their 1927 *Buck v. Bell* decision?

> Had you been living in the 1940s, would you have told fellow believers to stand down and pray while innocent

American citizens of Japanese descent were forced into internment camps causing many to lose their homes, businesses, and families—all because the Supreme Court said it was constitutional to do so in their 1944 *Korematsu v. United States* decision?

> Had you been living in 1944 Germany, would you have encouraged your fellow believers to simply stand down and pray while millions of Jews and other political dissidents, including many Christians, were rounded up and placed into internment camps where they were forced into slave labor and worked to death or were gassed and had their bodies cremated in massive furnaces?

Sadly, that is essentially what the majority of the church did then, and with the exception of a courageous minority, that is what the church is doing today. For the most part, today's church is standing down, doing precious little, while tyrants commit horrible atrocities in their very midst. Why? Partly because its leaders insist that Romans 13:1–5 demands *unlimited* submission.

The bottom line: we cannot commend all of the biblical and extrabiblical heroes for defying governmental authority when it is popular and suits our purposes and then play the hypocrite by insisting that everyone else should bow down to tyranny because our misinterpretation of the Bible says we must. Either Romans 13:1–5 demands *absolute* submission in **all** instances or there **are times** when defiance is not only *permitted* but *demanded* of Christians.

Chapter 2

An Exegesis of Romans 13:1–5

A Matter of Hermeneutics

Since Romans 13:1–5 is the *passage of choice* for those who teach *unlimited* submission to government and thus, creates the greatest amount of consternation and confusion for Christians, we will focus our discussion there. A proper understanding of Romans 13 will naturally determine how we interpret other similar passages. As it happens, once we properly understand Romans 13:1–5, the predominant *unlimited* submission position begins to unravel.

But, how can we know for certain what Romans 13:1–5 or any other passage of Scripture really communicates? Are we left to our own capricious and arbitrary interpretations? Is the true meaning determined by the loudest voice in the room?

Unfortunately, since most Christians have had little or no training in the "art" of proper Bible interpretation, they find themselves doing just that. Typically, they resort to simply taking a particular passage of Scripture and arbitrarily deciding what it says—often taking it out of context and reading into it an incorrect meaning (a dangerous practice known as Eisegesis—as opposed to Exegesis, the proper practice of allowing Scripture to speak for itself). Unfortunately, Romans 13:1–5 is a classic example.

Thankfully, we do not have to resort to guessing when it comes to determining what God means in His word. There is actually a scientific way to properly understand and interpret God's sometimes mysterious and difficult message. That science of properly interpreting the Bible, or any other written document for that matter, is known as Hermeneutics. By adhering to the rules of Hermeneutics we can avoid the mistakes commonly made in misinterpreting Scripture and can, thus, properly understand what the Apostle Paul was specifically saying to the Christians in Rome in the thirteenth chapter of Romans.

Although Hermeneutics is a great field of study all to itself, understanding a few of its key principles makes the task of interpreting Scripture immensely easier. Two of these principles that we will focus on here are the textual/historical context principle and the analogy of faith principle. Simply stated, these principles teach:

> ➤ **The textual/historical context principle:** the historical setting and the textual context of a particular passage must be considered in order to develop a proper understanding. One cannot simply pluck preferred verses or phrases out of context, both historically and textually, in order to teach something the passage is not actually saying.

> ➤ **The analogy of faith principle:** all Scriptures are divinely

inspired and are harmoniously united with no essential contradictions. No passage should be seen as standing alone but must be interpreted with the rest of Scripture in mind. In other words, Scripture should interpret Scripture. *The Westminster Confession* defines this principle like this: "The infallible rule of interpretation of Scripture is the Scripture itself: and therefore, when there is a question about the true and full sense of any Scripture (which is not manifold, but one), it must be searched and known by other places that speak more clearly." In his great work, *Systematic Theology*, Charles Hodge explains this principle by saying, "If the Scriptures be what they claim to be, the word of God, they are the work of one mind, and that mind divine. From this it follows that Scripture cannot contradict Scripture. God cannot teach in one place anything which is inconsistent with what He teaches in another. **Hence Scripture must explain Scripture**. If a passage admits of different interpretations, that only can be the true one which agrees with what the Bible teaches elsewhere on the same subject." [1] In short, if an interpretation of a particular passage does not harmonize with the totality of Scripture, that interpretation is incorrect.

The Context of Romans 13:1–5

Let us begin our examination of Romans 13:1–5 by going beyond chapter thirteen and carefully considering the context of the entire letter/book of Romans. By understanding when

---

1.   Hodge, Charles, *Systematic Theology*, Vol. 1, Introduction, Chapter VI, The Protestant Rule of Faith.

Paul wrote Romans, the reason he wrote it, and to whom he wrote it, we begin to take the first steps in developing a proper interpretation of the overall message of the book and of its individual sections in particular—including the much debated thirteenth chapter. As we perform this Hermeneutical exercise, it will become abundantly clear that Romans 13:1–5 does **not** teach that Christians owe *slavish, unlimited* submission to government.

Consider:

> **The time, place, and recipients of Romans:**

As its title indicates, Paul wrote the letter of Romans to the Church in Rome in A.D. 56–57 while he was in Corinth during his third missionary journey. At this time, Paul had not yet visited Rome and would not until he delivered the love offering he had collected for the impoverished believers in Jerusalem. Assuming the crucifixion and resurrection of Jesus occurred in approximately A.D. 33, then the church in Rome, if it had been started shortly thereafter, was only some twenty-three years old when Paul wrote them the letter we know today as the book of Romans. We do know that the Roman church dates back to at least A.D. 49 because the Roman historian Suetonius wrote that same year, "As the Jews were making constant disturbances at the instigation of Chrestus, he [Emperor Claudius] expelled them from Rome." (*The Lives of the Twelve Caesars*, Clau., XXV) Paul's letter would have been a wealth of new knowledge to these Roman believers since at this time the books that make up the New Testament were just beginning to be written.

25

Up until this time, the fledgling church in Rome had been completely dependent on the Holy Spirit's enlightenment of the Old Testament, information from travelers from Jerusalem, and those with particularly unique spiritual wisdom like the husband and wife team of Aquila and Priscilla. So Romans was truly a breath of fresh air to these early Christians.

> **The reason Paul wrote Romans:** In Romans 1:11, 15, Paul says that his reason for writing the letter was threefold: to encourage the Roman believers, establish their faith, and to impart to them some spiritual gift. As he wrote the thirteenth chapter, Paul must have been aware of some developing problems within the small church in Rome (chapters 12–15). It is plausible that Aquila and Priscilla, who had been deported from Italy by Emperor Claudius sometime between a.d. 49 and 52, may have informed Paul of the troubles in the church once they met up with him in Corinth (Acts 18:1–3). Having learned of the "troublesome" Jews in Rome who were the cause of Claudius's mass deportation of Christians and Jews, it is reasonable to conclude that Paul felt compelled to instruct the believers in Rome that they should co-exist with Roman rule as best they could while still honoring the Lord in order for the church to flourish. In doing so, Paul was most likely not intending to write a complete treatise on Christians and their interactions with government in all places and for all times, but was instead, trying to assist this young church as it struggled under the Roman system.

In a.d. 54, Nero had ascended to power after Claudius had experienced an untimely death from eating poisonous mushrooms and Paul would most likely have been aware of this development. It is **extremely important** to note that at the time Paul wrote Romans (a.d. 56–57), Nero's close adviser Seneca was still alive and having not yet retired, his counsel kept Nero from turning into the tyrant he would eventually become around a.d. 64 when Rome was decimated by a fire that Nero blamed on the Christians. Taking this into consideration alleviates the assumption by many that Paul was teaching that Christians must always *cooperate* with government—even when tyrants like the demonical Nero rule. Therefore, it is during Nero's "reasonable" rule in the middle of the first century, that Paul instructed the Roman believers to submit for "conscience's sake" so that the young church there could grow and the Gospel could spread—not necessarily because Christians had no right to stand up against evil or tyranny but in order that the "good news" could spread far and wide.

> **The theological implications of Romans:** Romans, as a whole, is a letter of instruction on doctrine and is central to the Christian faith—especially when it comes to the finer points of the Gospel. So when Paul tells the young Christians in Rome to submit to the Emperor's rule, which at the time was not yet as hostile to the Christian faith as it would become, we have to wonder what these believers were doing that necessitated Paul's admonition

to submit to their earthly rulers. Interestingly, although there are numerous unproven theories, the Scriptures are silent about the controversy. But one thing is certain—Paul believed that Christians should be known for their *general* respect for authority and in so doing would not only reflect their obedient posture toward God and human authority, but would also increase their ability to share the Gospel. Consequently, believers living under Roman rule would have been known as people of peace and would not have attracted the unwanted and unnecessary attention of the Roman authorities that were extremely wary of the new and growing Christian "sect."

With this in mind and before we examine the actual text of Romans 13:1–5, it is important to note that Paul was writing to first century Christians living under a dictatorship—a form of governance in which they had little or no influence. He was not directly addressing Christians living under a representative form of governance like we enjoy in the United States of America. Although this would seem obvious, it appears to be a point many who embrace the "unlimited submission" interpretation miss.

Factually, the Christians in Rome had no real voice in how their government functioned and had little choice but to get along with the Roman authorities as best as they could for the sake of the Gospel. It is within this narrow set of parameters that Paul was instructing these believers. Had Paul been writing to Christians living under a republican form of government like ours in America, it is reasonable to assume that he would have taken that into consideration as he wrote. Obviously, Paul would still instruct American Christians to respect and submit to authorities, but he might also adjust his instructions to include admonitions for them to exercise their constitutional rights in the face of tyranny just as he did when he asserted his rights as a Roman citizen in order to avoid an unjust beating by the Roman authorities (Acts 22:25).

Therefore, when applying the first five verses of Romans 13 in teaching submission to government, we must remember that in countries with a representative form of governance, like here in the U.S., there are options available to Christian citizens in dealing with their government that were not available to Christians living in Rome in the first century. Doing this, by the way, in no way diminishes the authority of Scripture—it simply keeps things within the proper historical/cultural context.

Did Paul and Peter Create a Scriptural Contradiction by What They Wrote?

In the first five verses of Romans 13, Paul clearly told the Christians in Rome to obey their Roman authorities. The text declares:

> "Let every soul be subject to the governing authorities. For there is no authority except from God, and the authorities that exist are appointed by God. Therefore whoever resists the authority resists the ordinance of God, and those who resist will bring judgment on themselves. For rulers are not a

terror to good works, but to evil. Do you want to be unafraid of the authority? Do what is good, and you will have praise from the same. For he is God's minister to you for good. But if you do evil, be afraid; for he does not bear the sword in vain; for he is God's minister, an avenger to execute wrath on him who practices evil. Therefore you must be subject, not only because of wrath but also for conscience' sake."

Considering that Paul wrote this passage by the inspiration of the Holy Spirit, the popular understanding today is that God is clearly telling His children that they owe *unquestioned* and *unlimited* submission to their governmental authorities. But is this what the text actually says? Before answering that question, it is important to remember that Paul is not the only Apostle who makes this argument. Peter took the same position when he wrote:

"Therefore submit yourselves to every ordinance of man for the Lord's sake, whether to the king as supreme, or to governors, as to those who are sent by him for the punishment of evildoers and for the praise of those who do good. For this is the will of God, that by doing good you may put to silence the ignorance of foolish men –"

—1 Peter 2:13–15, NKJV

If these two apostles were truly teaching *unlimited* submission to authority, then both of them were at complete odds with the biblical accounts we have already discussed when godly believers defied authority and were commended by God for doing so. If the modern "unlimited submission" interpretation of Paul and Peter's instructions is correct, then these two Apostles created an *actual* contradiction in Scripture—posing a huge problem for believers everywhere.

Ironically, by refusing to remain silent about their own faith, Paul and Peter were themselves often at odds with the authorities of their day. In fact, their defiance was so strident; it eventually led to their martyrdom. Therefore, it would seem extremely hypocritical for these two apostles to demand that the rank and file believer owes *unlimited* submission to government while they both lived and ministered a good deal of the time in open defiance to it.

Of course, these two Apostles were not hypocrites, and as we will see, if we compare what they wrote with other passages that commend believers for righteous defiance to tyranny, it becomes clear that they were both teaching a general truth that believers must be submissive to *proper* authority (Colossians 3:18–23, Hebrews 13:17, 1 Peter 5:5). But, when rulers/magistrates violate God's higher laws and become a "terror to good works," followers of Christ are not obligated to submit and must, instead, resist. Again, this is what happened with the Hebrew midwives, Daniel, etc. If these believers had submitted to the authorities of their day, they would have actually been disobeying God. The same principle applies to all believers in all times.

Thankfully, as we will see, an *apparent* biblical contradiction is not necessarily an *actual* contradiction. So, let us carefully examine what Paul *actually* says in Romans 13:1–5.

What Does the Text of
Romans 13:1–5 Actually Say?

Properly understanding what Paul meant in Romans 13 requires not only understanding what he *did* say but also understanding what he *did not* say. Significantly, Paul **does not** *actually* say that believers must always offer *unlimited* submission to *every* authority—even if that authority misuses their authority.

Again, remember that he was writing primarily to Christians living under a Roman dictatorship during the first century. Certainly, the first five verses of Romans 13 offers useful instruction for Christians in all times and places, but our application of these verses must be properly applied to those times and places. For example, Paul's instructions to the Christians in Corinth concerning women having their heads covered in church are not interpreted in a "wooden, literal" sense by most reasonable preachers/teachers today, but are interpreted within that particular cultural/historical context. Consequently, we do not force women to wear a head covering when entering our worship services. This same technique must be considered when interpreting Romans 13:1–5. This is not to say that we have the freedom to mold Scripture into whatever cultural shape we desire, but it is to say that passages of Scripture are sometimes written to address certain cultures, times, and places and may not directly apply to other cultures, times, and places in the same way.

A helpful way to properly interpret what Paul was actually teaching in Romans 13:1–5 about submission to government is to examine the text by focusing on the three aspects he emphasizes: the **position** government holds, the **purpose** government fulfills, and the **power** government wields. By doing so, the message becomes far more reasonable than the "unlimited submission to all authority" interpretation so popular in our day.

1. The Position Government Holds

In verse one, Paul writes that God is the source of all authority:

> "... For there is no authority except from God, and the authorities that exist are appointed by God."

In verse four, Paul twice declares that rulers/magistrates are God's ministers:

> "For he is God's minister to you for good. ... for he is God's minister, an avenger to execute wrath on him who practices evil."

Without embarking on a deep biblical dissertation about authority, Scripture teaches that all things, other than evil, emanate from God, the Creator and ultimate authority over all things. Authority, then, as a principle and as a position bestowed upon men, naturally finds its source in Him. And because God is the ultimate authority, all authority (heavenly and earthly) begins with and answers to Him. This is what Paul meant when he wrote, "For there is no authority except from God." Here he is emphasizing that no earthly authority intrinsically possesses that authority by birth or divine right but is granted that authority by God. Therefore, any earthly position of authority has loaned/borrowed authority from the Lord and must use it in a way that is congruent with what God intends.

Given this, when Paul then writes, "and the authorities that exist are appointed by God," he is saying that God, in His sovereign will, created a universe of law and order and appointed human government as the agent of His authority on earth to govern an unruly and fallen humanity. It naturally follows then, that if verse one declares that God ordains the *position* of authority, the *person* in authority would naturally be "God's minister" as verse four claims. Of course, this interpretation poses no difficulty when good, benevolent rulers/magistrates wield governmental authority. The problem arises when evil men like Nero, Hitler, Stalin, etc. possess the seat of authority. Is Paul saying that God appoints the Hitlers and Stalins of this world to be His "ministers"? This suggestion would seem to stretch credulity beyond the breaking point.

Although it is true that Scripture teaches that God sometimes appoints/allows evil men to rise to positions of power to discipline His people (this is very apparent in the history of the nation of Israel), does God divinely "pick" every person who holds a position of authority—including the evil ones? What about in nations/states with some form of democratic government where the citizens choose their own leaders? Does God sovereignly choose those as well? The short answer is "No!" At least that is the correct answer unless one is a blind fatalist who believes that every single thing that happens on earth throughout all time is directly ordained and manipulated by God.

Even though Scripture does teach that God is sovereign over all things, it does not teach that God ordains or causes all things. In fact, Scripture teaches that many things happen outside of the *perfect* will of God (consider Jesus' teaching in Matthew 19:7–9 that God *permits*, not *prefers* divorce). Certainly, nothing ever happens that threatens God or His sovereign will, but Scripture does teach that things contrary to God's will do happen. This means that God does not micromanage the universe to the degree that everything that happens is caused by Him. In the end, this would make God the author of sin—a concept that is completely unbiblical and untenable.

When in His sovereignty, God chose to create man in His own image, instead of making man a mere robot, God gave him a will of his own. It only makes sense then that God intends for man to exercise that will. In the course of exercising his will, God not only allows man to make choices, but also allows him to experience the consequences of those choices. In the end, man's life is a long string of choices through which he is intended to honor God. The late Baptist preacher Adrian Rogers was fond of saying, "You are free to choose but you are not free not to choose. Although you are free to choose, you are not free to choose the consequences of your choices." In some way, almost beyond our comprehension, God sovereignly works His will while allowing man certain latitude to make his own choices. Romans 8:28 brings some comfort to this dilemma by assuring us that God works all of this out for the good of His children.

Reason would then lead us to conclude that man's freedom of choice also extends into the arena of governance. When men have the privilege of choosing those who govern over them, they, not God, are responsible for the government they choose. For example, when ancient Israel demanded an earthly king, after warning them of the negative consequences, God granted their request. They unwisely chose Saul as their first king, and as God had warned, they paid dearly for their choice. In a representative form of government like our American republic, Americans have only themselves to blame if they choose poor leaders. Therefore, when Paul writes that "the authorities that exist are appointed by God," it would appear that he is referring primarily to the *position* of authority rather than the actual *person* who holds the seat of authority. Even so, once individuals are entrusted with authority, they are to function in accordance with God's principles and in doing so act as His "ministers for good."

It would be the height of inconsistency to teach that God directly places all who hold the reins of government into their positions. How could individuals like Nero, Hitler, or Stalin ever possibly be called "ministers of God"? We can therefore safely assume that Paul was not teaching that every person in authority is placed there by God and is therefore His minister for good. Instead, Paul was teaching that the position of authority in which men are placed makes them His ministers—if they use that authority properly. So according to Paul, God's definition of a *proper* government would be one that is led by a person whose actions are in accordance with biblical principles. It is under these conditions that a ruler can reasonably be called a "minister of God."

Unfortunately, this is not how it always works out. Because mankind is fallen and extremely sinful, evil individuals sometimes seize the reigns of government and wield its immense power to perpetrate evil. When this happens, as we will see, Scripture does not require that Christians obey these tyrants and violate God's higher laws—especially when they have legal means to resist such evil.

2. The Purpose Government Fulfills

In Romans 13:3–4, Paul proceeds to emphasize the purpose government fulfills:

> "For rulers are not a terror to good works, but to evil. Do you want to be unafraid of the authority? Do what is good, and you will have praise from the same. For he is God's minister to you for good. But if you do evil, be afraid; for he does not bear the sword in vain; for he is God's minister, an avenger to execute wrath on him who practices evil."

In calling rulers/magistrates "God's ministers," Paul qualifies this title by pointing out that the purpose of governmental authority is to be a minister for good. The proper purpose of government then, is to be "a terror to **evil** works" and to be "an avenger to execute wrath on him who practices **evil.**" This is the only condition under which a government official can conceivably be called "God's minister." If he is a "terror to **good** works" and "executes wrath on him who practices **good**," instead of being a minister for good, he has become a minister for evil.

According to Scripture then, the only kind of government deserving of the believer's *unlimited* submission is one that punishes doers of evil and rewards doers of good. Any ruler/magistrate that does the opposite, as Pastor Samuel West preached in 1776, "forfeits his authority to govern, and becomes the minister of Satan, and, as such, ought to be opposed." (See pages 112–114 for more from West.)

Once we understand this, Romans 13:1–5 takes on a very different meaning than the one ascribed to it by most modern preachers/teachers. This illustrates how emphasizing what Paul *actually* writes makes much more sense than reading something extra into the text that he did not write.

3. The Power Government Wields

Finally, in Romans 13:2–4, Paul discusses the power government wields:

> "Therefore whoever resists the authority resists the ordinance of God, and those who resist will bring judgment on themselves. … For rulers are not a terror to good works, but to evil. Do you want to be unafraid of the authority? … But if you do evil, be afraid; for he does not bear the sword in vain; for he is God's minister, an avenger to execute wrath on him who practices evil."

Here Paul points out the awesome power government wields—making it even more important that it is forced to fulfill its *proper* purpose. Since *proper* government operates as "God's minister," its ordinances would naturally be the ordinances of God and anyone who resists/disobeys those ordinances can expect only one thing—judgment. Being a "**terror** to evil," *proper* government should be feared because of its heavy and long arm. Paul goes so far as to say that *proper* government is an "avenger" who "executes **wrath**" on evildoers, even to the point of capital punishment ("he does not **bear the sword** in vain"). This is the reason Paul warns that all "must be subject … because of wrath."

Verse five concludes the passage with the admonition: "Therefore you must be subject, … for conscience' sake." This admonition emphasizes the importance of having a clear conscience—a critical component of a believer's spiritual walk. Paul reminds us that offering submission to *proper* authority (one that functions in accordance with God's principles) is our spiritual responsibility and obedience in this area helps to keep the believer's conscience clear. Additionally, when we submit to *proper* rulers/magistrates, our witness is strengthened as others, especially unbelievers, see us acting biblically toward godly authority. Of course, the converse is also true: if unbelievers see us appearing to agree and cooperate with improper, unjust authorities, we appear as hypocrites and damage our Christian witness.

Taken altogether, Romans 13:1-5 creates a very narrow definition of what a *proper* government is. Simply stated, a *proper* government is one that fulfills the original purpose God intended where doers of evil are punished and doers of good are rewarded. The obligation for a Christian's submission to authority falls within this narrow definition.

Chapter 3

Submission and Cooperation Is Not Always the Godly Option

Given the sickening sweet "let's all just get along" message of many modern spiritual leaders, it comes as a shock to many that Scripture **does not necessarily** teach that believers are commanded to get along with and cooperate with everyone. There are some people whose lives, worldview, and actions are so contrary to Scripture that we simply cannot align ourselves with them.

Oddly enough, Paul says this in the chapter *before* he writes his well known "submit to government" passage in Romans 13. In Romans 12:18, Paul wrote, **"If it is possible,** as much as depends on you, live peaceably with all men."

The "if it is possible" phrase of Romans 12:18 clearly indicates that, although peace/cooperation with all men is preferable and should be the goal of every believer (thus, the "as much as depends on you"), in a fallen world cooperation is not always possible. Certainly, we should do everything within our power to live peaceably with all, but once we have discovered this is not possible, we must do whatever we must, within biblical parameters, to remove ourselves from the influence/control of the unreasonable party.

This principle is illustrated in numerous passages throughout Scripture. For example, Abraham lived peaceably with his neighbors until they violated that peace by taking his nephew, Lot and his family as captives. Genesis 14 tells the story that when Abraham heard the news, he armed over three hundred of his men and fought a battle to free Lot, his family, and all of his personal possessions. A strong indicator of God's approval of Abraham's actions is that Melchizedek, the priest of "God Most High" (who is presented as a type of Christ in Hebrews 5–7), blessed Abraham after the battle and told him that God had actually delivered his enemies into his hand.

This is just one of multitudes of examples that reinforce Paul's teaching in Romans 12:18 that peace/ pacifism is not always the godly response. Space will not allow us to discuss how Joshua led the Israelites to conquest over the Canaanites, how King David fought the Philistines, how Nehemiah defied the enemies of God to rebuild the walls of Jerusalem, etc. What's more, this principle is not relegated to the Old Testament alone, but was even used by our Lord when He instructed his disciples how to conduct themselves as they evangelized. Matthew, Mark, and Luke all recorded the following statement of Jesus:

> "And whoever will not receive you nor hear your words, when you depart from that house or city, shake off the dust from your feet. Assuredly, I say to you, it will be more

tolerable for the land of Sodom and Gomorrah in the day
of judgment than for that city!"

—Matthew 10:14–15

So according to Jesus, there are limits as to how far we must
go in "accommodating" people even when we share the "good
news."

Then there is the somewhat cryptic statement our Lord
made in Luke 22. In Matthew 10:14–15, we find the story
of Jesus sending out His disciples on a mission to share the
"good news." It is in this passage that He told them to "shake
off the dust" of those who would not receive their message.
In sending them out, He also gave the explicit instruction for
them to, "Provide neither gold nor silver nor copper in your
money belts, nor bag for your journey, nor two tunics, nor
sandals, nor staffs; for a worker is worthy of his food" (Matthew
10:9–10). Months later, when He was preparing His disciples
to continue the Gospel ministry once He had ascended back
to the Father, He said:

> "And He said to them, 'When I sent you without money bag,
> knapsack, and sandals, did you lack anything?' So they said,
> 'Nothing.' Then He said to them, 'But now, he who has a
> money bag, let him take it, and likewise a knapsack; and he
> who has no sword, let him sell his garment and buy one.'"
>
> —Luke 22:35–36

Although there are numerous views of what Jesus meant when
He said, "he who has no sword, let him sell his garment and buy

one," it seems clear that He was, at the very least, preparing His disciples for a hostile environment in which they might, from time to time, be forced to defend themselves. Here Jesus seems to have been underlining the basic principle that cooperation/ submission is not always a viable option for God's people.

As has already been mentioned, Paul, himself, was unable to live peaceably with all men—including the governmental authorities. It is clear that he did not believe that God required him to "roll over" to every magistrate. Acts 21–22 tells how when Paul was in Jerusalem, the Jews were so offended at his message that they attempted to kill him. Had the commander of the Roman garrison at Jerusalem not intervened, the Jews may have very well succeeded. Once Paul was in the hands of the Roman soldiers, they bound him in preparation for scourging for causing such a ruckus. Rather than sheepishly bowing to an undeserved and illegal beating, Paul appealed to his Roman citizenship and stopped the soldiers in their tracks.

The next day, while defending himself before the Jewish high priest Ananias and his council (even though Paul did know initially that it was Ananias), Paul was slapped on the mouth by one of the Jewish officials at the command of the high priest. Again, rather than just sheepishly taking his lumps, Paul emphatically responded to Ananias, "God will strike you, you whitewashed wall! For you sit to judge me according to the law, and do you command me to be struck contrary to the law?" Even though Paul did not know that he was actually speaking to the Jewish high priest at the time, and once having learned this fact, apologized for speaking so bluntly to such a high ranking official, this episode illustrates that he obviously did not believe in rolling over and offering *unlimited* submission to authority. Was Paul respectful? Yes! Was he passive and groveling? No!

One is made to wonder how modern spiritual leaders and the rank and file believer can read passages like these and then come away with an *unlimited* cooperation/submission position. Unlimited submission is certainly not the proper, godly response when ungodly authorities are either allowing or committing unconscionable acts of evil—evils like Pharaoh's order to murder all of the Jewish baby boys, the Nazis' slaughter of the Jews, and the U.S. government's allowing preborn babies to be slaughtered in their mother's wombs.

It comes as quite the shock to many believers when they learn that Scripture **does not necessarily** teach that all authority is deserving of their submission. But a quick review of our discussion in chapter two shows that Paul makes a distinction between *godly* authority that deserves our submission and *ungodly/tyrannical* authority that does not. Again, according to Paul, the government deserving of a believer's submission is one that "executes wrath on him who practices evil" while "praising" those who do good:

> "For rulers are not a terror to good works, but to evil. Do you want to be unafraid of the authority? Do what is good, and you will have praise from the same. For he is God's minister to you for good. But if you do evil, be afraid; for he does not bear the sword in vain; for he is God's minister, an avenger to execute wrath on him who practices evil."
>
> —Romans 13:3–5, NKJV

45

Only when government functions properly can it reasonably be seen as "God's minister" and thus expect the full submission of Christians. Of course, when authorities function within their proper role, believers are obliged to submit. Conversely, when a government "executes wrath on him that practices *righteousness*" and "praises" evildoers, that government has no reasonable expectation of the submission of believers—especially when its actions bring Christians into conflict with God's higher laws.

There is an example from our War of Independence that illustrates this principle perfectly. One of the godly colonial pastors who, early on, had been against fighting the British was Congregationalist pastor Samuel Phillips Payson of Chelsea, Massachusetts. But when he heard that the British had attacked the colonists at Lexington on the morning of April 19, 1775, Payson experienced an immediate and permanent change of heart. The following account by Joel T. Headley describes Payson's reaction to the British attack as he fought the Red Coats in their retreat from Concord to Boston as they fled down what is known today as Battle Road on the afternoon of April 19:

"There, too, was the amiable and learned Payson, of Chelsea. He was so adverse to bloodshed and all the horrors of war that he had felt it his duty to preach patience and even submission. His bolder and more resolute brethren near him took such umbrage at this that they refused to let him preach in their pulpits. They wanted no conciliatory doctrines taught to their people. The brutal outrage at Lexington transformed this peaceful scholar and meek divine into the fiery, intrepid soldier, and seizing a musket he put himself at the head of a party, and led them forward to the attack. The gentle voice that had so long spoken only words of peace suddenly rung like that of a prophet of old. A body of British soldiers advancing along the road [from Concord back to Boston], he poured into them such a destructive volley that the whole were slain or taken prisoners. He was a man of peace and conciliation, but the first citizen's blood that crimsoned the green sward made a clean sweep of all his arguments and objections, and he entered with his whole soul into the struggle." [2]

Romans 13 Is Not the Only Bible Passage That Talks About Submission

It is important to remember that Romans 13:1–5 is not the only passage of Scripture that teaches the principle of submission to authority. Additionally, it is not just to *governmental* authority that Christians are instructed to submit—Scripture teaches that believers have a responsibility to submit to *all* in authority. For example:

> Ephesians 5:22 and 1 Peter 3:1 teach that wives should submit to the authority of their husbands.

> Exodus 20:12, Proverbs 6:20, 13:1, Matthew 15:4, and

2.   Headley, J. T., *The Chaplains and Clergy of the Revolution*. (New York: C. Scribner, 1864), Chapter 5, p. 60.

Ephesians 6:1 teach that children should submit to the authority of their parents.

> ‣ 1 Timothy 3:5, 5:17, Hebrews 13:7, and 1 Peter 5:3–6 teach that a congregation should submit to its pastor(s).

Even so, no reasonable person interprets these passages to teach that wives, children, and congregations owe *unlimited* submission to those authorities. All would agree that a wife has no biblical obligation to obey her husband if he asks her to steal something from the local convenience store for him. The same would apply to a son or daughter ordered by their parents to peddle drugs on the street to help the family's financial situation. A church congregation has no obligation to submit to an overbearing, sinful, or heretical pastor; on the contrary, they should rebuke and remove him. The fact is, anyone in authority demanding submission to unreasonable/ungodly demands must be ignored and disobeyed.

Oddly, even though most recognize that the *unlimited* submission position is ridiculous when applied to the above passages, they flip their logic when it comes to submission to government and take the *unlimited* position when dealing with passages like Romans 13:1–5. How do we explain this dichotomy in their thinking? Most likely they have been taught this contradictory theology by their pastors/teachers. Biblical consistency would dictate that a person's submission to governmental authority has the same limitations as a wife does to her husband, as children do to their parents, and as congregations do to their pastors. Submission to authority is always contingent upon how righteous and just the demands are that are made by the authorities.

A General Principle

Clearly, Romans 13:1–5 teaches a *general* principle—not one to be interpreted in a wooden, literal sense. This is actually common in Scripture and numerous passages must be understood in this way. For example, consider the oft quoted and misinterpreted passage of Proverbs 22:6. Many mistakenly believe this verse provides a *guarantee* to parents that if they "train up a child in the way he should go," they are *guaranteed* their child will grow into a godly adult. But when Solomon wrote this, he was stating a *general*, not *guaranteed*, truth. Proverbs 22:6 simply teaches the general truth that children who receive godly instruction are far more likely to grow into godly adults than those who receive no such instruction. Parents must understand that children have a will and are free to choose to obey or disobey God once they grow into adulthood—regardless of what they were taught when they were children. Most of us know sad stories of parents who raised their children to know and obey the Lord only to have them reject God's ways once they became adults. The late Dr. Adrian Rogers wrote this about properly interpreting Proverbs 22:6:

> "A proverb is a general principle that when generally applied will bring a general result. If you try to turn proverbs into promises, you'll lose your faith."[3]

3.   Rogers, Adrian, *Daily Heartbeat*, "Love Worth Finding," May 15, 2020

Understanding that Proverbs 22:6 offers a *general and conditional* promise prevents us from misinterpreting the passage and setting ourselves up for possible disappointment in both our children and God's word—thus illustrating the importance of carefully interpreting Scripture.

Just as in Proverbs 22:6, it would seem that Romans 13:1–5 offers a general, conditional command to submit to governmental authority when it is acting within its *proper* role. The numerous scriptural examples where God not only allowed, but applauded righteous defiance to governmental tyranny discussed previously prove this.

A critical point to understand: submission to human authority is secondary to submission to God's authority. There are times when, to remain faithful to God, believers must disobey human authority and face whatever consequences follow. This is what the early church did as recorded in the Book of Acts and this is the key to properly understanding Romans 13:1–5.

It Is No Small Thing to Resist Authority

Even though Paul makes it clear in Romans 12:18 that cooperation/submission is not always the correct option, defying authority, especially governmental authority, is a serious matter and any Christian who defies authority must never do so rashly or lightly. They must remember that they will ultimately answer to God for their actions and may even incur governmental wrath as a consequence of their defiance. History proves that there is an inherent risk involved when anyone resists an ungodly/evil government. The biblical heroes listed in chapter one were subject to the consequences of their acts of defiance and they fully accepted the outcome— regardless of whether God delivered them or not (this was the testimony of Shadrach, Meshach, and Abed–Nego in Daniel 3:16–18). Thus, when choosing to defy any authority, Christians must make certain they are acting in accordance with God's will and must be prepared for whatever consequences may follow.

Additionally, no one is suggesting that believers have the right under God to defy authorities acting *within* their proper roles and responsibilities. **Disagreeing** with the government is not necessarily **cause** for defiance. Defiance is only proper under the most extreme circumstances when obeying the government necessarily means disobeying God's principles and/or allowing evil to prosper. Only in tyrannous circumstances should defiance be chosen—and only in the most **extreme** circumstances should defiance ever become violent. Even then, when war is necessary, the rules of just war theory must be observed.

Thankfully, by the grace of God, unlike countless millions living under tyranny throughout the centuries, we Americans have seldom, if ever, had to face the difficult choice of defying our government. Even so, if today's cultural leftward drift continues, we may find ourselves facing this difficult choice in the very near future. If/when we do, let us not hide behind a faulty interpretation of Romans 13:1–5 but boldly stand for truth and justice—no matter the cost. In the end, believers not only have the *right,* they have the *responsibility* to defy ungodly/evil authority in the attempt to stop evil. This is especially true for those of us living in a *representative republic* like ours in which all political power ultimately rests with "the people."

Chapter 4

Our Best Chance for Proper Government Is Found in a Republic Like Our American Republic

There is no perfect template for creating the type of *proper* government Paul was talking about in Romans 13:1–5. Any government, even a monarchy/dictatorship, can properly fulfill God's design for government if it punishes the doers of evil and rewards the doers of good.

Even so, the type of government that holds the greatest promise for governing in the way God intends, where the authority becomes "God's minister" and is not "a terror to good works, but to evil," and where it functions as "an avenger to execute wrath on him who practices evil," is in a republic like our American republic. When rights are seen as gifts from God, not government, and where "the people" are the ultimate authority, not government, there is tremendous potential for that government to function properly.

Our American Republic

Those of us living in these United States of America are privileged to enjoy what precious few have in history—a government based on the "consent of the governed." Instead of giving us a monarchy or a dictatorship, our Founders/Framers gave us a representative republic governed by a written constitution. According to an attribution in the notes of Dr. James McHenry, a Maryland delegate to the Constitutional Convention of 1787, Benjamin Franklin, when exiting Independence Hall at the close of the Constitutional Convention, was asked by a woman, "Well, Doctor, what have we got—a Republic or a Monarchy?" According to McHenry, Franklin responded, "A Republic, if you can keep it." [4]

Our republic operates under the dictates of three primary documents: *The Declaration of Independence*, the individual constitutions of the various states, and the *U.S. Constitution*. Given the proper understanding and jurisdiction of each, we Americans, unlike the Apostles living under a Roman dictatorship, have a major voice in how we are governed. This fact greatly affects how we should apply Romans 13:1–5 to our lives here in the States. But in order to properly understand how Paul's teaching on government applies to us in our republican form of government, we must understand what a republic is and how it works.

What Is a Republic?

Merriam/Webster's Dictionary defines a republic as:

4.   McHenry, James, notes first published in *The American Historical Review*, Vol. 11, 1906, p. 618, included in *The Records of the Federal Convention of 1787*, ed. Max Farrand, Vol. 3, appendix A, p. 85 (1911, reprinted 1934), https://www. bartleby.com/73/1593.html.

"a government in which supreme power resides in a body of citizens entitled to vote and is exercised by elected officers and representatives responsible to them and governing according to law."

In attempting to explain our form of government, some mistakenly claim we are a democracy—a form of government in which a simple majority rules. Although this is a common mistake, it is exactly the kind of government the Framers were dead set on avoiding. Even though our form of governance employs the democratic process, the Framers knew that a pure democracy can be a cruel and most unfair kind of government in which a large minority (just under 50%) can be overwhelmed and steamrolled by the "tyranny of the majority" [5] (that may number just slightly over 50%). The Framers also knew that even though, as John Adams wrote, "the people are the best keepers of their liberty," [6] they will sometimes throw away their liberty under extreme circumstances. Therefore, the Framers worked to ensure that the liberties of the people were secured by a fairer and more just kind of governance than a simple democracy.

What they eventually designed was a republic that elected representatives of the people operating under a written constitution enact the "consent of the governed" into law. In

5. Adams, John, *The Works of John Adams, Second President of the United States*, Volume 6, Chapter 1: "A Defence of the Constitutions of Government of the United States of America," (Boston: Charles C. Little and James Brown, 1851), p. 63.
6. Ibid, Adams, John.

essence, the Framers created a hybrid republic of sorts. Men like Thomas Jefferson, John Adams, and Noah Webster called it a "representative republic." Others have called it a "democratic republic" or a "constitutional republic." One author called it a "constitutional federal representative democracy," [7] while another called it a "constitutionally limited representative democratic republic." [8]

Regardless of the title used, it is clear that the Framers were seeking to protect the unalienable rights of the people. Clifford Humphrey, authority on America's founding, wrote in *The Federalist*:

> "Our Founders did not believe that the people have a right to enact whatever laws the majority necessarily want, but, rather, that the people have a right to enact whatever laws the people as a whole think are just. That higher aspiration requires deliberation, but also time. The name the Founders most often gave to this form of government was 'republic.'
> … In a republic, the people are indeed sovereign and the majority has the democratic right to speak for the whole. But our Founders wisely limited the use of that democratic right with republican institutions in order to protect the people from 'the tyranny of their own passions [*Federalist*

7. Volokh, Eugene, "Is the United States of America a republic or a democracy?" May 13, 2015, https://www.washingtonpost.com/news/volokh-conspiracy/wp/2015/05/13/is-the-united-states-of-america-a-republic-or-a-democracy/.

8. Cunningham, Pat, "Is the United States a democracy or a republic? Actually, it's both" May 8, 2015, https://www.hillsdale.net/article/20150508/BLOGS/305089990.

63]." Thus our republic is democratic in that it is controlled by public opinion, but our Constitution requires patience and persistence for the people to express that opinion through elections. By filtering the people's judgment through elections over time, the Founders established a republic that would allow the people's best beliefs about what is just—not their immediate impulses for what they want—to guide the government. Such a deliberative process is best described as republican, not 'undemocratic.'"[9]

James Madison, the primary author of the U.S. Constitution, articulated the eighteenth century definition of a republic in *Federalist 39*:

"… we may define a republic to be, or at least may bestow that name on, a government which derives all its powers directly or indirectly from the great body of the people, and is administered by persons holding their offices during pleasure, for a limited period, or during good behavior."

This is the type of government we are graced by God to enjoy here in these United States—a republican government "of, by, and for the people." In addition to understanding that our government is a representative republic, it is also important that we understand the philosophical/spiritual atmosphere in which our government was created. In this way, we can better

---

9. "Sorry, liberals, but America is not a democracy, and it's better that way," Clifford Humphrey, Feb. 7, 2018, *The Federalist*, https://thefederalist. com/2018/02/07/sorry-liberals-america-not-democracy-better-way/.

understand the ideas that propelled those who founded and framed our republic.

Our Republic Was Not Born in a Philosophical/Spiritual Vacuum

Contrary to what modern leftists would want us to believe, our American republic was not birthed in a philosophical/spiritual vacuum. The American colonies of the seventeenth–eighteenth centuries were undeniably and predominantly Christian in their philosophy and religious persuasion. Obviously, not every American at the time of our founding/framing claimed to be a born-again Christian, but most had a profound respect for the God of the Bible and *generally* held to Christian values. This explains, to a large degree, why the republican principles employed in our founding worked so effectively—at least for some time. Sadly, having strayed far from our moral roots, today our founding documents seem to be failing us. Interestingly John Adams actually predicted this possibility when he wrote, "Our Constitution was made only for a moral and religious people. It is wholly inadequate to the government of any other." [10]

Because of the fallen nature of man and his craving for personal promotion and power and as the American culture

---

10. John Adams, *The Works of John Adams, Second President of the United States: with a Life of the Author, Notes and Illustrations, by his Grandson Charles Francis Adams* (Boston: Little, Brown and Co., 1856), Vol. 9. Chapter: To the Officers of the First Brigade of the Third Division of the Militia of Massachusetts.

becomes increasingly immoral and irreligious, the footings of our once great republic have been eaten away and we are now in the process of jettisoning our founding documents and the principles they enshrine. And just as Adams warned, to the extent we have rejected Christian values, our founding documents are increasingly seen as antiquated and have been misinterpreted, abused, ignored, and now seem incapable of protecting our unalienable rights.

But, it was not always this way. Regardless of how pluralistic and divergent parts of our Union have become in the twenty-first century, especially in regard to faith and morality, it is simply beyond dispute that our Founders and Framers were heavily influenced by the Christian sentiment of their day. Americans were clearly "Christianity/Bible friendly" when our republic was born. Again, this is not to say that every American in 1776 was a born-again Christian, but biblical values/morality were embraced by the majority.

This being the case, history and experience taught the Framers that only a *moral* and *religious* people (they were referring to Christianity) are capable of self-governance and that an immoral and irreligious culture will require extreme governmental oversight. Benjamin Franklin articulated this concept when he said, "Only a virtuous people are capable of freedom. As nations become corrupt and vicious, they have more need of masters." [11] Many of our Framers openly communicated the critical role Christianity plays in securing our rights—here are a few examples:

11. Franklin, Benjamin, *The Writings of Benjamin Franklin*, Vol. 9, (Macmillan, 1906), p. 569, Letter: To Messrs. The Abbes Chalut and Arnaud, Philadelphia, April 1787.

> **George Washington** (Commander of Continental Army, first President of U.S.):

"Of all the dispositions and habits which lead to political prosperity, Religion and morality are indispensable supports. In vain would that man claim the tribute of Patriotism, who should labour to subvert these great Pillars of human happiness, these firmest props of the duties of Men and citizens. ... where is the security for property, for reputation, for life, if the sense of religious obligation desert the Oaths, which are the instruments of investigation in Courts of Justice? And let us with caution indulge the supposition, that morality can be maintained without religion. ... Reason and experience both forbid us to expect that National morality can prevail in exclusion of religious principle." [12]

> **John Adams** (first Vice President of U.S., 2nd President of U.S.):

"We have no government armed with power capable of contending with human passions unbridled by morality and religion. Avarice, ambition, revenge, or gallantry, would break the strongest cords of our Constitution as a whale goes through a net. Our Constitution was made only for a

---

12. Washington, George, "Farwell Address, Sept. 19, 1796," University of Virginia, The Washington Papers, http://gwpapers.virginia.edu/documents_gw/farewell/transcript.html

moral and religious people. It is wholly inadequate to the government of any other." [13]

> **Elias Boudinot** (President of Second Continental Congress, NJ Congressman in the first, second, & third Congresses, founder of American Bible Society):

"[I have] an anxious desire that our country should be preserved from the dreadful evil of becoming enemies to the religion of the Gospel, which I have no doubt, but would be introductive of the dissolution of government and the bonds of civil society." [14]

> **John Quincy Adams** (statesman, diplomat, lawyer, and sixth U.S. President):

"The greatest glory of the American Revolution was that it bound together in one indissoluble bond the principles of Christianity and the principles of civil government." [15]

---

13. John Adams, *The Works of John Adams, Second President of the United States:* with a Life of the Author, Notes and Illustrations, by his Grandson Charles Francis Adams (Boston: Little, Brown and Co., 1856), Vol. 9. Chapter: To the Officers of the First Brigade of the Third Division of the Militia of Massachusetts.
14. Boudinot, Elias, *The Age of Revelation or The Age of Reason Shewn To Be An Age of Infidelity*, 1801, Preface, p. XXII.
15. Speech delivered in 1837 during a Fourth of July celebration at Newburyport, Massachusetts.

> **Samuel Chase** (signer of the Declaration of Independence, U.S. Supreme Court Justice):

"By our form of government, the Christian religion is the established religion;" [16]

This theme was also reflected in the official policies of the day. For example, as Americans began to move westward into relatively uninhabited lands, recognizing that these areas needed proper governance and would most likely eventually become states, Congress drew up a governing document in 1787 for those regions called *The Northwest Ordinance*. This document stated in part: "Religion [they meant Christianity], morality, and knowledge being necessary to good government and the happiness of mankind, schools and the means of education shall forever be encouraged."

Even though the evidence of the Christian leanings of the Founders and Framers seems overwhelming to most, by the mid 1800s, some began to reject this notion, arguing that America's Founders and Framers never intended that our government reflect or support Christian values. Pushing forward with this misguided theory, these secularists protested the use of tax dollars to pay Christian chaplains who served in numerous areas of the government—specifically, they objected to paying Christian chaplains for the U.S. House and Senate. Even though the practice of paying Christian chaplains from public funds had roots tracing back to George Washington and

16. Chase, Samuel, Opinion as Chief Justice of Maryland in *Runkel v. Winemiller*, 1799

the Continental Army, the argument was essentially that, by paying these chaplains with money from taxpayers, the U.S. government was violating the First Amendment of the U.S. Constitution by establishing a state church.

> *Note:* Today's Americans completely misunderstand the phrase "establishment of religion" found in the First Amendment. The prohibition actually refers to an "established" or official church like the English had with the Church of England. It was not intended to prevent religious activities like the display of nativity scenes on public property, prayers being offered in public facilities or by public officials, the Ten Commandments being posted on/in public buildings, etc. Its purpose was to prevent the government from forcing all citizens to recognize or belong to a national church—a far cry from a cross being erected on a desolate piece of public property in an American desert or a nativity scene on the courthouse lawn in some small town in a southern State.

This complaint moved Congress to initiate a thorough study of our history to determine the *original intent* of our Founders and Framers. The Judiciary Committees of both the U.S. House of Representatives and the U.S. Senate conducted thorough investigations and eventually released their findings. In those reports, it was stressed that, although the Founders and Framers never intended to so unite church and state that a theocracy would result, the evidence clearly showed that they did intend that *general* Christian values would be promoted and protected by the government. Not surprising, the findings of both committees were essentially the same. Consider the following excerpts from those reports:

> ### The House Judiciary Committee Report:

"The reason more generally urged [by those opposed to official chaplains], is a danger of a union of church and State. If the danger were real, we should be disposed to take the most prompt and decided measures to forestall the evil, … But we deem this apprehension entirely imaginary; and we think any one of the petitioners must be convinced of this on examination of the facts. … The sentiment of the whole body of American Christians is against a union with the State. A great change has been wrought in this respect. At the adoption of the Constitution, we believe every State, certainly ten of the thirteen, provided as regularly for the support of the church, as for the support of the government: … Down to the Revolution, every colony did sustain religion in some form. It was deemed peculiarly proper that the religion of liberty should be upheld by a free people. Had the people, during the Revolution, had a suspicion of any attempt to war against Christianity, that Revolution would have been strangled in its cradle. At the time of the adoption of the Constitution and the amendments [Bill of Rights], the universal sentiment was that Christianity should be encouraged—not any one sect [denomination]. Any attempt to level and discard all religion, would have been viewed with universal indignation. The object was not to substitute Judaism or Mahomedanism [Islam], or infidelity, but to prevent rivalry among sects [Christian denominations] to the exclusion of others. The result of the change above named is, that now there is not a single State that, as a State, supports the gospel. … This change has been made silently and noiselessly, with the consent and wish of all parties, civil and religious. It seems to us that the men who would raise the cry of danger in this state of things, would cry fire on the thirty-ninth day of a general deluge. … If there be a God who hears prayer—as we believe there is—we submit, that there never was a deliberative body that so eminently needed the fervent prayers of righteous men as the Congress of the United States." [17]

> ## The Senate Judiciary Committee Report:

"[F]rom the beginning, our government has had chaplains in its employment. If this had been a violation of the Constitution—an establishment of religion—why was not its character seen by the great and good men who were coeval with the government—were in Congress and in the Presidency when this constitutional amendment [First Amendment] was adopted? … Our fathers were true lovers of liberty, and utterly opposed to any constraint upon the rights of conscience. They intended, by this amendment, to prohibit 'an establishment of religion' such as the English

---

17. *Reports of Committees of the House of Representatives Made During the First Session of the Thirty-Third Congress* (Washington: A. O. P. Nicholson, 1854).

church presented, or anything like it. But they had no fear or jealousy of religion itself, nor did they wish to see us an irreligious people; they did not intend to prohibit a just expression of religious devotion by the legislators of the nation, even in their public character as legislators; they did not intend to send our armies and navies forth to do battle for their country without any national recognition of that God on whom success or failure depends; they did not intend to spread over all the public authorities and the whole public action of the nation the dead and revolting spectacle of atheistical apathy. Nor so had the battles of the Revolution been fought, and the deliberations of the Revolutionary Congress conducted. On the contrary, all had been done with a continual appeal to the Supreme Ruler of the world, and a habitual reliance upon His protection of the righteous cause which they commended to His care.

The petitioners say, 'A national chaplaincy, no less than a national church, is considered by us emphatically an establishment of religion.' In no fair sense of the phrase have we a national chaplaincy; in no sense in which that phrase must be understood when connected, as it is by the petitioners, with a 'national church.' A national church implies a particular church selected as the church of the nation, endowed with peculiar privileges, or sustained or favored by the public in preference to other churches or religious societies. Of such a church we have no semblance, nor have we any such chaplaincy. We have chaplains in the army and navy, and in Congress; but these are officers chosen with the freest and widest range of selection—the law making no distinction whatever between any of the religions, churches, or professions of faith known to the world. Of these, none, by law, is excluded; none has any priority of legal right. True, selections, in point of fact, are always made from some one of the denominations into which Christians are distributed; but that is not in consequence of any legal right or privilege, but by the voluntary choice of those who have the power of appointment.

This results from the fact that we are a Christian people—from the fact that almost our entire population belong to or sympathize with some one of the Christian denominations which compose the Christian world. And Christians will of course, select, for the performance of religious services, one who professes the faith of Christ. This, however, it should be carefully noted, is not by virtue of provision, but voluntary choice. We are Christians, not because the law demands it, not to gain exclusive benefits, or to avoid legal disabilities, but from choice and education; and in a land thus universally Christian, what is to be expected, what desired, but that we shall pay a due regard to Christianity, and have a reasonable respect for its ministers and religious solemnities?" [18]

Summary

Scripture teaches that it is impossible to live at peace with ev-

---

18. *The Reports of Committees of the Senate of the United States for the Second Session of the Thirty Second Congress, 1852–53*, (Washington: Robert Armstrong, 1853), p. 3.

eryone. Therefore, there are times when righteous separation or resistance is not only allowed but required.

It is also simply beyond debate that those who founded and then framed our republican form of government did so in a "Christian" environment and intended that the country/government they were founding/framing would reflect Christian principles. They clearly believed this was the only way to secure the peoples' unalienable rights. Although what they created is by no means perfect, it has provided Americans with the greatest potential in history to enjoy their unalienable rights—specifically, "life, liberty, and the pursuit of happiness."

So, in properly applying Romans 13:1–5 in America, Christians must recognize that we live in a republic that was designed around Christian values and morals—not a pagan dictatorship under which the Apostles lived. Only by understanding this can we hope to avoid making the mistake of teaching that Americans owe unlimited submission to their governmental authorities.

But some ask how we should apply Romans 13:1–5 today since Christianity unfortunately no longer has the influence in America it once did. With our American culture as deeply polarized philosophically/religiously as it is and with our differences seemingly irreconcilable, how can we possibly respect the rights and beliefs of all sides? The answer is found by returning to the mechanism in our form of government that solves the problem—federalism.

Chapter 5

Federalism Is the Answer

In review, to properly apply Romans 13:1–5 in our republic, American Christians must consider the following truths:

1. Romans 13:1–5 teaches a *general* principle of limited submission to governmental authority when it is acting *properly and lawfully* within God's original framework for the purpose of government.

2. In 1776–1783, God, in His sovereign providence, allowed a representative republic to be formed by the original thirteen colonies in North America.

3. This republic was not formed in a philosophical/spiritual vacuum. The predominant belief when our republic was formed was Christian and Christian values are reflected in our founding documents that outline our basic American understanding of right and wrong and the proper role of government.

4. Based upon the principles laid out in America's primary

founding documents: *The Declaration of Independence*, the constitutions of those original thirteen states (and eventually the other thirty-seven states), and the U.S. Constitution, our government derives its just powers from the "consent of the governed."

5. In our representative form of government, THE PEO-PLE are the governing authorities and government officials are elected to represent the people. (A very different kind of government than that faced by those in the New Testament era.)

6. To the extent the government appointed by the American people adheres to the principles laid out in our founding documents, the American citizens (including Christians) must submit to that government. Americans are not bound to submit to the whims of governing individuals/bodies just because they hold official positions of governmental authority—those individuals/bodies must act lawfully or they are to be resisted and ultimately replaced by the people.

We Weren't Always As Pluralistic As We Are Today

Even though it is clear that our founding/framing generations generally embraced a Christian worldview, regrettably, that is no longer the case in numerous states/regions of our Union. Modern America is unquestionably a pluralistic society, deeply divided by philosophical/religious beliefs. The philosophical/ spiritual divide is so great today that our culture may be irreconcilably divided with the different sides too far apart for reconciliation. We have certainly reached the place where no "one size fits all" solutions from the federal government in Washington D.C. can satisfy the different factions of our very diverse culture (as if that was ever the case). For example:

> How is it possible to reconcile those who believe a preborn human is nothing more than a blob of tissue with those who believe life begins at conception and that the preborn baby is human from the very moment of conception and any intentional ending of that life is, by definition, murder?

> How is it possible to reconcile those who *reject* our founding principles of "life, liberty, and the pursuit of happiness," individual responsibility, capitalism, etc. as originally understood with those who hold to the *original intent* of the Framers and to the original definition of such terms?

> How is it possible to reconcile those who reject the original meaning of the freedoms protected by the First Amendment with those who hold to their meaning as understood in the late 18th century?

> How is it possible to reconcile those who believe guns commit crimes and that gun ownership should be strict-

ly controlled by the government or completely abolished with those who believe criminals commit crimes and that gun ownership for self-defense is an unalienable right given by God?

You get the picture.

With the leftward spiritual drift of the American Christian church over the past one hundred years, a *spirit of secularism* has swept in, denying any *official* governmental recognition of religion (especially Christianity) and seems hell-bent on eradicating all vestiges of our Christian heritage and faith. Adherents to this *new brand of tolerance* insist that Christian beliefs and values have no place in the public square and should be kept completely private—all while secular humanist beliefs (recognized by American courts as a religion) are enacted into law and forced upon everyone. If these secularists have their way (as they are in many places), how must Christians, who can only submit to a **proper government** described by Paul in Romans 13:1–5, respond when, in good conscience, they cannot submit to the ungodly decrees/laws forced upon them by secular humanists? The answer is found in revisiting the governmental principle that was the genius of our founding—a principle known as *federalism*.

Federalism Is the Answer

In great contrast to the Roman dictatorship under which the New Testament church lived, our system of government was based on the organizing principle of *federalism*. Federalism is a system of government in which two different levels of government govern the same area/people. The *national* or *federal* government is generally responsible for larger territorial and foreign issues while the state governments govern the issues of local concern. Additionally, the individual states also retain their autonomy from one another so that the cultural distinctives of one state remain unmolested by the cultural distinctives of the others. In this way, the cultural/philosophical/religious beliefs of the citizens of the states/regions are protected from a "one size fits all" overreaching federal government. In this type of government, both the federal government and the state governments have the power to make laws and both retain a certain level of autonomy.

In this system of "dual sovereignty" the U.S. Constitution embraces, the states delegated (loaned) certain powers to the federal government while retaining all other powers not *expressly* designated to the federal government by the Constitution. By its very definition then, federalism creates an atmosphere of "tension" between the individual state governments and the federal government, thus placing a "check" on the expansion of federal power over the states. This is exactly what the Framers intended.

James Madison, known as the "chief architect of the U.S. Constitution," writing in *Federalist #45*, provides a succinct and salient definition of federalism, as the Framers understood it in 1776–1788:

> "The powers delegated by the proposed Constitution to
> the federal government are few and defined. Those which

are to remain in the State governments are numerous and indefinite. The former will be exercised principally on external objects, as war, peace, negotiation, and foreign commerce; with which last the power of taxation will, for the most part, be connected. The powers reserved to the several States will extend to all the objects which, in the ordinary course of affairs, concern the lives, liberties, and properties of the people, and the internal order, improvement, and prosperity of the state."

Generally, the states intended for the new federal government they were creating to have very limited powers—"enumerated powers" found in Sec. I, Art. 8 of the U.S. Constitution. The Framers believed that the government closest to the people should be the strongest. Therefore, the states, where the people actually lived, worked, raised families, etc., were understood by the Framers to retain the greatest amount of power and that the powers delegated (not surrendered) to the federal government by the states would be "few and defined." This would ensure that if the federal government ever abused its power by overreaching and became tyrannical or totalitarian, the people in the states would be able to interpose and stop it. Although this may be a revolutionary thought in the twenty-first century, it is completely consistent with the principles of our founding.

Thomas Jefferson, the chief author of the *Declaration of Independence*, strongly agreed with Madison that the federal government's authority was very limited and that the states retained a great deal of sovereignty. Consider his comments in three of his letters:

> **February 15, 1791 letter to George Washington:**

"I consider the foundation of the Constitution as laid on this ground: That 'all powers not delegated to the United States, by the Constitution, nor prohibited by it to the States, are reserved to the States or to the people.' To take a single step beyond the boundaries thus specially drawn around the powers of Congress is to take possession of a boundless field of power, no longer susceptible of any definition." [19]

> **August 13, 1800, letter to Gideon Granger, politician, lawyer, Postmaster General under President Jefferson:**

"Our country is too large to have all its affairs directed by a single [federal] government. Public servants at such a distance, and from under the eye of their constituents, must, from the circumstance of distance, be unable to administer and overlook all the details necessary for the good government of the citizens and ... will invite the public agents to corruption, plunder, and waste." [20]

> **June 12, 1823, letter to William Johnson, nominated to the U.S. Supreme Court by Jefferson in 1804:**

"[T]he capital and leading object of the Constitution was to leave with the states all authorities which respected their

---

19. Library of Congress, https://www.loc.gov/resource/mtj1.013_0984_0990/?st=text
20. Library of Congress, https://www.loc.gov/resource/mtj1.022_0365_0367/?st=list

own citizens only, and to transfer to the U.S. those which respected citizens of foreign or other states: ... Can any good be effected by taking from the states the moral rule of their citizens, and subordinating it to the general authority [federal government], or to one of their corporations, which may justify forcing the meaning of words, hunting after possible constructions, and hanging inference on inference, from heaven to earth, like Jacob's ladder? Such an intention was impossible, and such a licentiousness of construction and inference, if exercised by both governments, as may be done with equal right, would equally authorize both to claim all powers, general and particular, and break up the foundations of the Union. ... I believe the states can best govern our home concerns, the general government our foreign ones. I wish therefore to see maintained that wholesome distribution of powers established by the con-stitution for the limitation of both: & never to see all offices transferred to Washington, where further withdrawn from the eyes of the people, they may more secretly be bought and sold as at market."[21]

It is important to remember that the states formed the federal government—not the other way around. The Framers who were sent to what became the Constitutional Convention were there as representatives of the people in their respective states. Presumably, they had no intention of surrendering their home state's sovereignty to a more powerful, central

---

21. Library of Congress, https://www.loc.gov/item/mtjbib024682/

government—especially since they had just fought a bloody and costly eight-year war freeing themselves from just such a governmental arrangement. It makes no sense that they would have, after winning that war, turned around and immediately placed themselves under a similar type of government they had just thrown off. Therefore, the Framers created a federalist, republican form of government in which the people in the individual states would be the strongest line of defense against an overreaching federal government.

In *Federalist Paper #33,* Alexander Hamilton wrote:

"If the federal government should overpass the just bounds of its authority and make a tyrannical use of its powers, the people, whose creature it is, must appeal to the standard they have formed, and take such measures to redress the injury done to the Constitution as the exigency may suggest and prudence justify."

In his *Virginia Resolution* of 1798, James Madison actually called federal overreach "evil," and declared that the states not only had the **right**, but the **responsibility** to "arrest" it:

"[I]n case of a deliberate, palpable, and dangerous exercise of other powers, not granted by the said compact, the states who are parties thereto, have the right, and are in duty bound, to interpose for arresting the progress of the evil. ..."

We must understand that America was not a "monolithic nation" at its founding—it was comprised of thirteen distinct and sovereign colonies uniting together to resist an overreaching central government located at that time in England. But even though they united for mutual protection, the colonies had no intention of surrendering the entirety of their sovereignty to the alliance—and the same goes for the states when they formed the U.S. federal government a few years later after the War of Independence was won. (See the complete *Federalist Papers 33 & 45*, the *Virginia Resolution,* & the *Kentucky Resolution.*)

In 1776, before the war ever started, the Second Continental Congress had boldly stressed this independent sovereignty of the States in the *Declaration of Independence*:

> "That these united Colonies are, and of Right ought to be Free and **Independent States** [emphasis mine], that they are Absolved from all Allegiance to the British Crown, and that all political connection between them and the State of Great Britain, is and ought to be totally dissolved."

Nothing Has Changed

Nothing has changed legally since those words were penned. The "Free and Independent States" have **never** *officially* surrendered their sovereignty to the federal government in Washington D.C. Although, some do argue that the War Between the States, fought from 1861–65, abolished state sovereignty and firmly established, once and for all, the supremacy of the federal government. If these people are correct and indeed the states actually did lose their sovereignty with the ending of the War and the ratification of the thirteenth and fourteenth

Amendments, why do we continue to recognize, fund, and operate state governments? Are the states now just Washington D.C.'s *helpers*? Why waste billions each year operating state governments and agencies if they are really nothing more than redundancies of the federal government and are immediately trumped by that federal government whenever there are disagreements? It would seem more efficient to simply abolish all of the states, shred individual state constitutions, sell off state capitols and agency properties, lay off all of those elected to state government positions, redesignate the previous states as new federal districts, and open up federal offices in each of those new federal districts. So, in my state of Oklahoma for example, instead of having a state government, we would simply have an office for the federal District of Oklahoma located quite possibly in Oklahoma City. All state officials would be unnecessary and could possibly seek employment as federal agents in the new federal District of Oklahoma. Then, Washington D.C. could be the unabashed, ultimate authority over everything and no longer have to do the "dance" around the states who actually have no "real" power—only that which is allowed by the federal government. But, that would completely destroy the United States of America as originally founded and as we know it. Additionally, it would forever seal our fate and place us under one, monolithic government with little to no "real" recourse because of its size and distance from the people.

Thankfully, the states actually still exist and function officially as governments, so it naturally follows then, that given the fact that the states only *delegated* the federal government's powers to it, they can, in cases of serious abuse, take those delegated powers back. If this is not true, we are truly no longer a Union of Sovereign States joined together by a common compact (the U.S. Constitution) and we should change our name from the United States of America to something else that truly reflects what we really are and prepare for a very different kind of governance from what we have known for over two centuries.

But, based upon our Founders/Framers, our founding principles, documents, and agreements, the individual states remain and have never been, and are not now, subservient to Washington D.C. If Washington oversteps its enumerated powers, "the free and independent" people of the states have no obligation to obey. This *revolutionary* thought was actually articulated by Thomas Jefferson in his 1798 *Kentucky Resolution*:

> "... that whensoever the general [federal] government assumes undelegated powers, its acts are unauthoritative, void, and of no force ..." [22]

Sadly, over the years, the states have allowed the federal government to "assume" so many "undelegated powers," specifically through the federal courts, that we must honestly wonder how could anyone say today that Washington D.C.'s powers are "few and defined" as Madison and the other Framers intended? Our federal government has so utterly violated the *Madisonian* definition of federalism (especially in the courts) that it has practically lost its legitimacy to govern. Only by

---

22. Jefferson, Thomas, *Kentucky Resolution*, 1798.

restoring a proper and dignified relationship between the state and federal governments can we step away from the *tyranny of an overreaching federal government* and actually honor the original intent of our founding principles and the sacrifice and blood that was shed to secure them.

So, when Romans 13:2 warns that resisting governmental authority is tantamount to resisting God and that those who do so will be judged, believers **are truly sinning** and **will face the appropriate judgment** from God if they refuse to submit to their government when it is acting within its *proper, godly* role. But, in a representative republic (where *the people*, under God, are the ultimate "authority") and where federalism is the form of government, if the state or federal governments, or any agencies of those governments, i.e. the U.S. Supreme Court, issue unrighteous, unreasonable laws/decrees that violate the consent of the people and the righteous principles of God, **it is the government** that is "resisting the ordinance of God"—not the people. In fact, in this scenario, the people **must resist** that government. In this case, it is the governmental authorities who are "bringing judgment/condemnation upon themselves"—not the people who are simply exercising their God-given, unalienable rights.

So for example, in 1973 when the U.S. Supreme Court ruled in *Roe v. Wade* that it is constitutional to murder preborn babies in their mother's wombs, in living out the true spirit of Romans 13:1–5 in a system of federalism, the states (certainly those where moral citizens are in the majority) should have stepped in, pointed out that the Court did not even have the jurisdiction to rule on such a subject, and then have refused to enforce such an ungodly decree within their respective state borders. Additionally, a moral person who embraces basic, historic morality (especially the Christian) is bound by Scripture and moral duty to ignore *Roe* and do all within their power to lawfully see that it is ignored in their state. After all, God's higher law commands: "Thou shall not murder"—and there is certainly no more accurate term for killing a preborn child than murder.

Essentially, it is really no more complicated than that. In our representative republic, if the people in some state believe that abortion is wrong, they have the responsibility to stop it and no government, be it state, federal, or the U.S. Supreme Court, has the authority to force that evil upon them. If the government will not cooperate, then according to the *Declaration of Independence,* the people have the authority to "alter, abolish, or throw off" their government and establish a new one that will reflect their will. This is what our ancestors actually did in 1776. This is not sinful disobedience to Scripture, it is not rebellion, nor is it anarchy—it is living in accordance with our founding documents and our finest American traditions. Just imagine how our Founders/Framers would have reacted to *Roe v. Wade*—they would probably have fought another War of Independence!

No One Size Fits All

In our modern pluralistic culture, federalism is actually the only and most peaceful way to deal with the ever-increasing polarization of our population. The days of Washington D.C.

being able to pass a "one size fits all" law concerning a highly controversial moral issue that will satisfy the beliefs of the people in all fifty states is gone—as if that day ever really existed. The people, worldviews, and cultures of the individual states are simply too divergent (and growing more and more so every day) for a *monolithic, national* government to be able to address all of their concerns. This is what Thomas Jefferson was saying in his August 13, 1800, letter to Gideon Granger when he wrote, "Our country is too large to have all its affairs directed by a single [federal] government."

Federalism recognizes this and makes it possible for the states to govern their people better than an *all-powerful* central government in D.C.—sometimes thousands of miles removed from the people it is attempting to govern. Thomas Jefferson actually articulated this concern over two hundred years ago:

> "I wish therefore to see maintained that wholesome distribution of powers established by the constitution for the limitation of both [state and federal governments]: and never to see all offices transferred to Washington, where further withdrawn from the eyes of the people, they may more secretly be bought and sold as at market." [23]

> "Our country is too large to have all its affairs directed by a single [federal] government. Public servants at such a distance, and from under the eye of their constituents, must, from the circumstance of distance, be unable to administer and overlook all the details necessary for the good govern-

---

23. Thomas Jefferson letter to George Washington, Feb. 15, 1791.

ment of the citizens and ... will invite the public agents to corruption, plunder, and waste." [24]

So again, an all-powerful federal government was never the *true* intent of the Framers. They intended for the federal government to deal mostly with disputes between the states and issues of foreign entanglement and they intended the states to govern issues that in the "ordinary course of affairs" affected the "lives, liberties, and properties of the people, and the internal order, improvement, and prosperity of the state."

The beauty of a federalist system is that each individual state government can govern in a way that best reflects the majority of its citizens. For those who do not feel well represented by their state governments, there is always the option to move to another state where the opinion of the majority more closely reflects their own. In this scenario, Christians, and non-Christians who at least embrace Christian values, can live out the principles outlined in Romans 13:1–5 without having to violate their consciences. This was the original intent of our Founders/Framers and this is the only peaceful solution for our modern, deeply divided culture.

---

24. Thomas Jefferson letter to Gideon Granger, Aug 13, 1800

Chapter 6

Were Our Founders and Framers Sinning When They Declared Their Independence from England?

Most of those who fled European tyranny and sailed to North America in the seventeenth century did so driven by their faith and their search for freedom. Although the Separatists, more commonly know today as "the Pilgrims," were not the first to travel to the New World to find freedom, they are probably the most well known—especially to Christians. Yet, these faithful Christians became famous by defying the English government.

Believing that the English Anglican Church, the official Church of England, was too far gone for reformation, these believers (the Pilgrims) determined to *separate* rather than to participate in what they saw as a vain attempt to *purify* their decadent state church (thus the titles: Separatists and Puritans). The famous 1843 Robert W. Weir painting now hanging in the rotunda of the U.S. Capitol captures the moment the Pilgrims were embarking on their long and perilous journey from Holland to North America. In the painting, the little band of Christians are pictured on board their first ship, the *Speedwell,* kneeling around their pastor, John Robinson, and their church elder, William Brewster, who is holding a Geneva Bible. And yet, just a decade before, these committed Christians had broken the laws of England to illegally flee to Holland without the King's permission—all to escape the control of the English King and his Church. Obviously, the Pilgrims did not hold to the *limited submission* interpretation of Romans 13:1–5.

After sailing over sixty days crossing the Atlantic, nearing the northeastern coast of North America, the Pilgrims and their little ship were driven off course by a storm. Landing near modern-day Provincetown, Massachusetts, these Christian "Separatists" eventually chose to establish their colony across the bay in what is modern Plymouth, Massachusetts. The fact that they did not have a charter from the King permitting them to settle there seemed of little concern at that point. Having made up their minds to settle there anyway, before disembarking from their ship, they took the time to write their *Mayflower Compact*, one of the earliest governing documents ever written in North America. In their *Compact*, they declared:

"We, whose names are underwritten, the loyal subjects of our dread Sovereigne Lord, King James, ... **having undertaken, for the glory of God, and advancement of the Christian faith**, and honour of our king and country, a voyage to plant the first colony in the Northerne parts of Virginia, doe by these presents solemnly and mutually in the presence of God and one of another, covenant and combine ourselves together into a civill body politick, for our better ordering and preservation, and furtherance of the ends aforesaid; and by virtue hereof to enacte, constitute, and frame such just and equall laws, ordinances, acts, constitutions and offices, from time to time, as shall be thought most meete and convenient for the generall good of the Colonie unto which we promise all due submission and obedience." (emphasis mine)

So the Pilgrims were missionaries? But how could they have claimed to be "advancing the Christian faith" while defying the British government in the process if they believed Romans 13:1–5 teaches unlimited submission to government? Were the Pilgrims hypocrites? Of course not! They simply did not embrace our modern unlimited submission interpretation of Romans 13.

Interestingly, every fourth Thursday of November, preachers across America honor the faith of these devout icons of Christian faith and liberty. But since the majority of these same preachers believe and preach/teach that Romans 13:1–5 teaches unlimited submission to government, their Thanksgiving celebration is in reality a colossal contradiction—because according to the "unlimited submission" interpretation of Romans 13:1–5, the Pilgrims were rebels who wantonly disobeyed the Scriptures. Ironically, while these preachers honor the Pilgrims, they condemn our eighteenth century Framers for essentially doing the same thing the Pilgrims had done a little over a century before. What's more, these preachers are quick to condemn anyone today who dares to even suggest that there are times when it is appropriate and even biblical to resist or defy governmental authority.

The fact is, in the 1770s, men like George Washington, John Adams, James Madison, and Thomas Jefferson, felt just as compelled and justified to defy the tyranny of the English government as the Pilgrims had before them. But how is it that some modern Christians condemn Washington and his ilk for refusing to submit to the English government but celebrate the Pilgrims for their defiance? This is duplicity at its best!

This is the reason it is so important that we revisit the thinking of the Founders/Framers. We must understand why they felt so compelled and justified to do what they did—especially considering that so many of them claimed to be Christians and were certainly aware of what Romans 13:1–5 teaches.

"Rebellion To Tyrants Is Obedience To God"

Once the Colonies had declared their independence, the Continental Congress tasked Thomas Jefferson, John Adams, and Benjamin Franklin with designing a national seal for the new government. The three presented their design to the Congress for adoption on August 20, 1776. Many Americans are surprised today to learn that the seal they proposed was comprised of a circle with a drawing in its center depicting the drowning of Pharaoh's army in the Red Sea, with Moses and the Israelites looking on while the Divine pillar of fire/smoke hovers overhead. Around the perimeter of the circle was the phrase "Rebellion To Tyrants Is Obedience To God." Although sadly, their design was never adopted, it offers clear evidence that Jefferson, Adams, and Franklin definitely did not believe that citizens owed *unlimited* submission to their government and certainly did not view defiance to tyrannical government as sinful rebellion.

This principle was so important to that generation that they enshrined it in our national birth certificate—the *Declaration of Independence*. That hallowed document actually opens with the following statement of respectful defiance to governmental authority gone awry:

> "When in the Course of human events, it becomes necessary for one people to dissolve the political bands which have connected them with another, and to assume among the powers of the earth, the separate and equal station to which the Laws of Nature and of Nature's God entitle them,"

Later in the document, Thomas Jefferson wrote these revolutionary words: "Governments are instituted among Men, deriving their just powers from the consent of the governed," thus declaring that the seat of governmental authority is "the People." From our earliest history, Americans have fervently believed that proper government answers to the people—not the other way around.

Knowing full well the fallen nature of mankind and having personally experienced the heavy hand of the tyranny of an overreaching government, Jefferson and his committee felt it necessary to prescribe the remedy available to the people should their government ever cease to fulfill its proper role:

"That whenever any Form of Government becomes destructive of these ends, it is the Right of the People to alter or to abolish it, and to institute new Government, laying its foundation on such principles and organizing its powers in such form, as to them shall seem most likely to effect their Safety and Happiness."

Given this, it is important to understand that the Framing generation was no collection of lawless rebels. To the contrary, they held law and authority in high regard and had long labored to find reasonable solutions to their differences with the English King and Parliament. Unfortunately, the English authorities were unmoved by the American colonists' many petitions—many of which are enumerated in the *Declaration* itself.

Once the patience of the Americans was exhausted, and with no peaceful solution on the horizon, they reticently, but boldly declared their independence and went about forming their new government—all the while understanding that war could be the result. Were they wrong to do so? The *unlimited submission* crowd believes they were. Most Americans believe they weren't and have celebrated their defiance every Fourth of July for over two centuries to prove it. Just imagine how different life in America (and the whole world for that matter) would be today had the Framing generation offered unlimited submission and bowed to British tyranny. Even though a good portion of the citizens living in 1770s America embraced Christian principles, when they realized that the British were unwavering in their hardline position, they did not hesitate to defy their authority.

Many Americans are surprised today to discover that many of the preachers in the colonies helped to lead out in the independence effort. In addition to pastoring their churches, a good number also served in the government of their respective colonies (they had not yet been deceived by the "separation of church and state" myth/lie). Some of them were appointed by their colonies to represent them in the Continental Congress. For example, John Witherspoon, Presbyterian preacher and President of what later became Princeton University, served in the very Continental Congress that voted to separate from England. Preachers like Lutheran/Anglican preacher, Peter Muhlenberg, who served in the Virginia House of Burgesses, was a personal friend of George Washington and Patrick Henry, and served as a general on Washington's staff, recruited men from their churches and communities, and led them off to fight on the battlefields of our War of Independence. They made such an impact that they earned the hatred of the British who dubbed them the "Black Regiment"—referring to the black robes they wore when they preached. These committed men of God strongly believed that when a government usurps its authority, it becomes *improper* and relinquishes its right to govern. Convinced that this is exactly what the British government had done, they believed it was their duty to resist and replace it—just as Thomas Jefferson had articulated in *The Declaration*. (For more information about these Patriot Preachers, see the author's book and video, *Bringing Back the Black Robed Regiment*, both of which can be ordered at danfisherbrr.com.)

Duke University historian Alice Baldwin, Ph.D, discussed the beliefs of this generation in her 1928 book, *The New England Clergy and the American Revolution*. In it, Baldwin describes the prevailing philosophy of government in America's founding era:

> "Probably the most fundamental principle of the American constitutional system is the principle that no one is bound to obey an unconstitutional act.... No single idea was more fully stressed, no principle more often repeated, through the first sixty years of the eighteenth century, than that governments must obey law and that he who resisted one in authority who was violating that law was not himself a rebel but a protector of law." [25]

Dr. Baldwin was absolutely correct and our history provides conclusive evidence that resistance to tyranny has always been in the finest traditions of our American culture—a culture with strong Christian roots. Yet ironically, it was not until preachers and politicians started preaching their *unlimited submission to government* message in the twentieth century that Americans began to embrace a slavish posture toward government. The Framers would be rolling over in their graves if they could see us now!

---

25. Baldwin, Alice M. *The New England Clergy and the American Revolution.* (New York: F. Ungar Pub., 1958, chapter 12, p. 169.

Chapter 7

The Tyranny of the Courts

Tyranny, no matter the source, is still tyranny.

We must always properly understand and apply Scripture—regardless of our situation. The present state of our U.S. court system, especially the U.S. Supreme Court, coupled with the incorrect belief of most Americans that the Supreme Court is the superior of our three branches of government and decides what is the law of the land, necessitates that we, now more than ever, correctly apply Romans 13:1–5. Unfortunately, the courts have been the tool most used by the *statists* to expand the power of government and to move our republic closer to tyranny. (*Statist* is a term coined by constitutional expert and conservative talk show host Mark Levin designating those who believe that government, not the people, is the seat of governmental power) Therefore, it is critical that we understand the role of the courts and what the Framers originally intended. Only then can we properly apply Romans 13 to our situation and engage in the fight for righteousness as God requires.

Government Must Be "Checked"

It is first important to understand that the Framers, fearing the encroaching nature of government over the rights of men, intentionally designed numerous checks and balances into our system of government. This was a critical point to them since, for the most part, they understood the wickedness of the human heart and the fact that man, rather than being intrinsically good, is fallen and sinful. They also understood that without restraints, men typically devolve into debauched behavior, and if they have the power, tend to become tyrants. John Adams made this point when he wrote:

> "To expect self-denial from men, when they have a majority in their favor, and consequently power to gratify themselves, is to disbelieve all history and universal experience; it is to disbelieve Revelation and the Word of God, which informs us, the heart is deceitful above all things, and desperately wicked. ... Such exalted virtue never yet existed in any large body of men and lasted long; ... There is no man so blind as not to see, that to talk of founding a government upon a supposition that nations and great bodies of men, left to themselves, will practice a course of self-denial, is either to babble like a new-born infant, or to deceive like an unprincipled impostor."[26]

Knowing that fallen men generally seek to accumulate power and force their will upon others, the Framers created a government of three complimentary and yet, competing branches—the executive, legislative, and judicial. This,

---

26. Ibid, Adams, John, *The Works of John Adams*, "A Defense of the Constitution of the United States of America," pp. 61–62.

they reasoned, would keep any one branch from usurping its authority over the other two. If any branch attempted to take over, the other two branches would naturally team up against the offending branch to protect themselves.

These individual branches, sometimes referred to by the Framers as departments, were given unique and specific responsibilities and powers reserved only to that particular branch. This division in the branches is known as "the separation of powers" and is critical for the health and survival of the republic. The principle in layman's terms can best be described as each branch *staying within its own lane.*

Fearing the prospect that this principle of separation of powers might be ignored in the future, George Washington warned in his 1796 *Farewell Address*:

"It is important, likewise, that the habits of thinking in a free country should inspire caution in those entrusted with its administration, to confine themselves within their respective constitutional spheres, avoiding in the exercise of the powers of one department to encroach upon another. The spirit of encroachment tends to consolidate the powers of all the departments in one, and thus to create, whatever the form of government, a real despotism."

In *Federalist 48*, James Madison echoed Washington's warning:

"It is agreed on all sides, that the powers properly belonging to one of the departments ought not to be directly and completely administered by either of the other departments.

It is equally evident, that none of them ought to possess, directly or indirectly, an overruling influence over the others, in the administration of their respective powers. It will not be denied, that power is of an encroaching nature, and that it ought to be effectually restrained from passing the limits assigned to it."

It is clear that the Framers intended the executive, legislative, and judicial branches to function within their realm of responsibility with relative ease and jurisdiction. But it is equally clear that they also wanted to restrict each branch from intruding into the powers and responsibilities of the other branches.

When considering the judiciary, it must be remembered that it is only one of three branches. It is also interesting to note that in establishing the judiciary, the Constitution uses less space than it does to establish either of the other two branches—Article I establishes the legislative branch, using ten sections, Article II establishes the executive branch using four sections, and Article III establishes the judiciary using only three sections. Given the attention the Framers gave to the Legislative branch in the Constitution, it would appear that they considered it the most important branch. This is likely because the legislative branch is closest to the people and is the one most accountable to them.

Additionally, it must be noted that the Constitution actually only establishes the Supreme Court—it is left to Congress to create additional federal courts as needed. (Article III, Section 1: "The judicial Power of the United States, shall be vested in one supreme Court, and in such inferior Courts as the Congress may from time to time ordain and establish.")

It seems obvious that the Framers did not hold the Supreme Court in the highly elevated position in which it is held today (the inordinate level of power the Court wields today is causing disastrous affects to our republic). One of the outward signs of this fact is that, until 1935, the Court did not have its own building and met in the basement of the Capitol building beneath the House of Representatives and the Senate.

But once the Court conferred upon itself the power of judicial review, especially as it is understood today, it began to accumulate more and more power—power that now threatens the rights of the people. Although it is agreed that the judiciary has expertise and responsibility in the area of determining constitutionality, it does not possess the final word on all things constitutional. If it does, the executive and legislative branches, whose members also take an oath to uphold and defend the Constitution, could eventually be usurped and made subservient to the Court. Dr. Larry Arnn, President of Hillsdale College, Hillsdale, Michigan, warns, "... the power of judicial review does not make the courts superior to the other branches, which have an equal obligation to interpret and uphold the Constitution."[27]

So contrary to what has become common belief, the Supreme Court's opinions are not more important or authoritative than the opinions of the executive and legislative branches. The problem is most people do not understand this and mistakenly believe the Supreme Court holds ultimate

---

27. Arnn, Larry, Hillsdale College online courses, *"Marbury v. Madison:* Judicial Review, https://online.hillsdale.edu/courses/the-us-supreme-court.

authority and power—after all, the word "supreme" is in its name. Making matters worse, the average citizen is completely unaware of how this misunderstanding endangers our republic and our freedoms. Abraham Lincoln, though often guilty of abusing his executive powers himself, understood this fact early in his presidency. In his first Inaugural Speech, Lincoln emphasized the danger of allowing the Supreme Court's opinion to be the ultimate, final word (emphasis mine):

> "I do not forget the position assumed by some that constitutional questions are to be decided by the Supreme Court, nor do I deny that such decisions must be binding in any case upon the parties to a suit as to the **object of that suit**, while they are also entitled to very high respect and consideration in all parallel cases by all other departments of the Government. And while it is obviously possible that such decision may be erroneous in any given case, still the evil effect following it, being **limited to that particular case**, with the chance that it may be overruled and never become a precedent for other cases, can better be borne than could the evils of a different practice. At the same time, the candid citizen must confess that if the policy of the Government upon **vital questions affecting the whole people is to be irrevocably fixed by decisions of the Supreme Court**, the instant they are made in ordinary litigation between parties in personal actions **the people will have ceased to be their own rulers**, having to that extent practically **resigned their Government into the hands of that eminent tribunal**. Nor is there in this view any assault upon the court or the judges.

It is a duty from which they may not shrink to decide cases properly brought before them, and it is no fault of theirs if others seek to turn their decisions to political purposes."

Lincoln was right in his understanding that the court's decisions must necessarily be limited to the particular cases they address. If, as he reasoned, in "vital questions" that affect everyone, the court has the power to dictate to the people, then we no longer operate by the "consent of the governed" but by the *will of the courts.*

Ignoring Lincoln's warning, Americans have allowed the Court's jurisdiction to expand well beyond what the Constitution specifies and what the Framers originally intended, threatening the very liberties it was created to protect. Surprisingly, even a number of the Framers seem to have been blind to this potential danger themselves. For example, Alexander Hamilton revealed his own naivety concerning the potential threat of a runaway judiciary when he wrote in *Federalist 78*:

"... the judiciary, from the nature of its functions, will always be the least dangerous to the political rights of the Constitution; because it will be least in a capacity to annoy or injure them. The Executive not only dispenses the honors, but holds the sword of the community. The legislature not only commands the purse, but prescribes the rules by which the duties and rights of every citizen are to be regulated. The judiciary, on the contrary, has no influence over either the sword or the purse; no direction either of the strength or of the wealth of the society; and can take no active resolution whatever. It may truly be said to have neither FORCE nor WILL, but merely judgment; and must ultimately depend upon the aid of the executive arm even for the efficacy of its judgments."

Unfortunately, Hamilton could not have been more wrong. As Larry Arnn points out:

"Today's Supreme Court holds great power to shape American society, contrary to the founders' view of the Court as the "least dangerous" branch. ... Judicial decisions have done much to advance a Progressive agenda that poses a fundamental threat to liberty. ... To put this power in the hands of judges who believe the Constitution does not have a fixed meaning, poses a serious threat to freedom." [28]

Among the original Framers, none feared federal overreach more than Thomas Jefferson. Jefferson was particularly concerned that the judiciary posed the greatest threat to the liberty of the people. Comments from three of his letters adequately illustrate this fear:

> **September 11, 1804, letter to Abigail Smith Adams, the daughter of Pres. John Adams:**

"... nothing in the Constitution has given [the judiciary] a right to decide for the Executive, more than to the ex-

---

28. Ibid, Arnn, Larry, Hillsdale College, *"Marbury v. Madison."*

ecutive to decide for them. Both magistracies are equally independent in the sphere of action assigned to them ... the opinion which gives to the judges the right to decide what laws are constitutional, and what are not, not only for themselves in their own sphere of action, but for the Legislature & Executive also, in their spheres, would make the judiciary a despotic branch."

> **May 28, 1807, letter to John Wayles Eppes, Jefferson's son-in-law who served as a congressman and senator:**

"But all this will show the original error of establishing a judiciary independent of the nation, and which, from the citadel of the law, can turn its guns on those they were meant to defend, and control and fashion their proceedings to its own will."

> **March 4, 1823, letter to William Johnson, nominated to the U.S. Supreme Court by Jefferson in 1804:**

"... there is no danger I apprehend so much as the consolidation of our government by the noiseless, and therefore unalarming, instrumentality of the Supreme Court."

Jefferson's fear was well grounded. A study of history confirms that by their very nature, courts and tribunals have wielded great power throughout the centuries, often violating the basic rights of the people.

In 1819, Thomas Jefferson and Judge Spencer Roane, a

Justice on the Virginia Court of Appeals (eventually becoming the Virginia Supreme Court), were debating the role and powers of the American judiciary. In making the point that he believed the judiciary was the superior branch of the three, Judge Roane quoted from the *Federalist Papers* claiming, "The judiciary is the last resort in relation to the other departments of the government." On September 6, 1819, Jefferson responded in a letter:

> "If this opinion be sound, then indeed is our constitution a complete *felo de se* [suicide pact]. For intending to establish three departments, co-ordinate and independent, that they might check and balance one another, it has given, according to this opinion, to one of them alone, the right to prescribe rules for the government of the others, and to that one too, which is unelected by, and independent of the nation. ... The constitution, on this hypothesis, is a mere thing of wax in the hands of the judiciary, which they may twist and shape into any form they please. It should be remembered, as an axiom of eternal truth in politics, that whatever power in any government is independent, is absolute also; in theory only, at first, while the spirit of the people is up, but in practice, as fast as that relaxes. Independence can be trusted nowhere but with the people in mass. They are inherently independent of all but moral law."

Jefferson then proceeded to emphasize that the judiciary had no more power or right to interpret the U.S. Constitution than any of the other two branches of government:

> "My construction of the constitution is very different from that you quote. It is that each department is truly independent of the others, and has an equal right to decide for itself what is the meaning of the constitution in the cases submitted to its action; and especially, where it is to act ultimately and without appeal."

On September 28, 1820, Jefferson wrote to William Charles Jarvis, a farmer, merchant, and diplomat whom he had appointed as consul to Lisbon, Portugal, in 1802. In his letter, Jefferson once again opined about the danger he believed the judiciary posed to liberty:

> "[Y]ou seem to consider the judges as the ultimate arbiters of all constitutional questions: a very dangerous doctrine indeed and one which would place us under the despotism of an Oligarchy. Our judges are as honest as other men, and not more so. They have, with others, the same passions for party, for power, and the privileges of their corps. Their maxim is *'boni judicis est ampliare jurisdictionem,'* [good justice is broad jurisdiction; i.e., it is the duty of a good judge to enlarge the jurisdiction of his court] and their power the more dangerous as they are in office for life, and not responsible, as the other functionaries are, to the elective control. The Constitution has erected no such single tribunal knowing that, to whatever hands confided, with the corruptions of time and party its members would become

despots. It has more wisely made all the departments co-equal and co-sovereign within themselves."

Sadly, today Thomas Jefferson's fears have come to fruition. Modern Americans are truly living under what Jefferson termed the "despotism of an Oligarchy." This is an easy enough fact to prove. One need only cite a few of the many unconscionable, immoral, and unconstitutional U.S. Supreme Court decisions to prove his case:

> *Dred Scott v. Stanford,* **1857,** when the Supreme Court ruled that Blacks were not humans but property that could be sold and purchased like common chattel.

> *Buck v. Bell,* **1927,** when the Supreme Court ruled that those deemed "unfit" by the courts to reproduce can be forcibly sterilized without their consent.

> *Korematsu v. U.S.,* **1944,** when the Supreme Court ruled that American citizens can be deprived of their unalienable rights simply because of their ancestry.

> *Roe v. Wade,* **1973,** when the Supreme Court ruled that a woman has the constitutional right to abort (murder) her unwanted preborn child.

> *National Federation of Independent Business v. Sebelius,* **2012,** when the Supreme Court ruled that the government

has the right to force American citizens to purchase health insurance.

> *Obergefell v. Hodges,* **2015,** when the Supreme Court reserved the right to define marriage and ordered states to defy their own state constitutions and issue marriage licenses to same-sex couples.

In all of these rulings (and more like them coming with every passing year), even though the Court ruled immorally and unconstitutionally, because of our misunderstanding of the power and role of the judiciary and because of our misunderstanding of Romans 13:1–5, these egregious decisions have been allowed to be imposed upon Americans as "law"—even though the judiciary cannot even make laws, that being the sole responsibility of the legislative branch. While these injustices have taken place, most believers have done little substantively, to stop them because, in most cases, they have been muzzled by a misinterpretation of Romans 13:1–5.

Here is the great danger: if the courts can determine who is "unfit" to reproduce and is therefore worthy of sterilization, if the courts can force American citizens into internment camps because of their ancestry, if the courts can tell us what we must purchase, is there any area of our lives they cannot control if they are so inclined? Essentially, if they are the "ultimate arbiters of all constitutional questions," their power is only limited by their good will. As the Framers knew in their day and as we all know today, there will always be unscrupulous individuals who so crave the

power of the bench that they will work their way through the court system until they reach the pinnacle of the U.S. Supreme Court. Once they do, what can we do if, when they perpetrate tyranny from the bench, their rulings are final and unalterable? If the "unlimited submission" interpretation of Romans 13 is correct, then in this scenario, there is nothing Christians can do but endure the tyranny, pray, and hope for a better day. Is this really what God has in mind? Of course not! Tyrants must be resisted. The Church, the body of Christ, just as it was in our founding era, is an essential firewall against such tyranny—but only if it engages. Unfortunately, most American Christians have been taught and therefore believe that Romans 13:1–5 forbids any and all resistance to governmental authority—so they do nothing as government runs roughshod over the rights of the people.

Dr. Larry Arnn warns, "Returning the Court to its proper role as a bulwark of limited, constitutional government is essential for the preservation of liberty." Christians must stop bowing in blind submission to the Supreme Court and hiding behind a misinterpretation of Romans 13:1–5. Our republic's future depends on the church's willingness to insist on proper, just government.[29]

29. Op. cit., Arnn, Larry, Hillsdale College, "Marbury v. Madison.

Chapter 8

American Preachers Did Not Always Believe That Romans 13:1–5 Demands Unlimited Submission to Government

One of the reasons our eighteenth century ancestors saw things they way they did was the considerable influence the Christian church and its preachers had on the culture. As counterintuitive as it may be to the predominant view of Christians in the twenty-first century church, there was a time in America when many preachers/pastors did not preach *slavish*, *unlimited* submission to government. Instead, they stood in their pulpits railing against British tyranny and urging their congregations to stand against it. Consequently, as we noted earlier, the British hated them, calling them the "Black Regiment" and attempted to silence them by any means necessary. A good number of these preachers gave their lives in a cause they believed was as righteous as the Gospel ministry to which they had been called.

These "patriot preachers" were confident that if the British government was intent on trampling the God-given, unalienable rights of the people, it had forfeited its legitimate claim as a "punisher of evil," and had, itself, *become that evil.* Convinced that the illegitimate actions of the King and Parliament were forcing them into conflict, they believed that the Church had a responsibility to do something about it. And since they believed that God had not forbidden the Colonists from defending themselves, numerous pastors and spiritual leaders of high moral character/reputation encouraged a stand. It seemed abundantly clear to them that standing **for** what is right sometimes requires standing **against** what is wrong. Their conclusion: if the sword could be justly used to punish an evil individual, it could also be justly used to punish an evil ruler/government as well—be he King, member of Parliament, or British soldier.

The following sermon excerpts are from some of these leading American preachers from that era and illustrate how many of them understood the subject of submission to governmental authority in their day:

> **Joseph Lathrop's** sermon, "A Sermon On a Day Appointed for Publick Thanksgiving," preached in Springfield, Massachusetts, December 14, 1787:
>
> "Perhaps it will be asked, 'Is there no case in which a people may resist government?' Yes, there is one such case; and that is, when rulers usurp a power oppressive to the people, and continue to support it by military force in

contempt of every respectful remonstrance. In this case the body of the people have a natural right to unite their strength for the restoration of their own constitutional government." [30]

> **Elizur Goodrich's** sermon, "The Principles of Civil Union and Happiness Con idered and Recommended," preached in Hartford, Connecticut, in 1787:

"When a constitutional government is converted into tyranny, and the laws, rights and properties of a free people are openly invaded, there ought not to be the least doubt but that a remedy is provided in the laws of God and reason, for their preservation; nor ought resistance in such case to be called rebellion." [31]

> **Jonathan Mayhew's** 1749–50 multi-discourse sermon, "A Discourse Concerning Unlimited Submission and Non-Resistance to the Higher Powers":

"No government is to be submitted to, at the expense of that

30. Lathrop, Joseph, "A Sermon On a Day Appointed for Publick Thanksgiving," Sandoz, *Political Sermons of the American Founding Era: 1730–1805*, 2 vols, Foreword by Ellis Sandoz (2nd ed. Indianapolis: Liberty Fund, 1998). Vol. 1. Chapter: 29.

31. Goodrich, Elizur, "The Principles of Civil Union and Happiness Considered and Recommended," preached in Hartford, CN, 1787, Sandoz, *Political Sermons of the American Founding Era: 1730–1805*, 2 vols, Foreword by Ellis Sandoz (2nd ed. Indianapolis: Liberty Fund, 1998). Vol. 1. Chapter: 31.

which is the sole end of all government—the common good and safety of society. ... The only reason of the institution of civil government and the only rational ground of submission to it is the common safety and utility. If therefore, in any case, the common safety and utility would not be promoted by submission to government, but the contrary, there is no ground or motive for obedience and submission, but for the contrary. ... [But] the duty of unlimited obedience, whether active or passive, can be argued neither from the manner of expression here used, nor from the general scope and design of the passage [Romans 13:1–7].

"If rulers are a terror to good works, and not to the evil; if they are not ministers for good to society, but for evil and distress, by violence and oppression; if they execute wrath upon sober, peaceable persons, who do their duty as members of society; ... it is plain that the apostle's argument for submission does not reach them; they are not the same, but different persons from those whom he characterizes; and who must be obeyed according to his reasoning. ...

"Rulers have no authority from God to do mischief. If those who bear the title of civil rulers, do not perform the duty of civil rulers, but act directly counter to the sole end and design of their office; if they injure and oppress their subjects instead of defending their rights and doing them good; they have not the least pretense to be honored, obeyed and rewarded, according to the apostle's argument. ... It is blasphemy to call tyrants and oppressors, God's ministers. They are more properly the messengers of Satan to buffet us. ... The argument here used [Romans 13] no more proves it to be a sin to resist such rulers, than it does, to resist the devil, that he may flee from us. ... No rulers are properly God's ministers, but such as are just, ruling in the fear of God. ... [N]o civil rulers are to be obeyed when they enjoin things that are inconsistent with the commands of God: All such disobedience is lawful and glorious; ... All commands running counter to the declared will of the supreme legislator of heaven and earth, are null and void: And therefore disobedience to them is a duty, not a crime. ...

"The king is as much bound by his oath, not to infringe the legal rights of the people, as the people are bound to yield subjection to him. From whence it follows, that as soon as the prince sets himself up above law, he loses the king in the tyrant: he does to all intents and purposes, un-king himself, by acting out of, and beyond, that sphere which the constitution allows him to move in. And in such cases, he has no more right to be obeyed, than any inferior officer who acts beyond his commission. The subject's obligation to allegiance then ceases of course: and to resist him, is no more rebellion, than to resist any foreign invader. ...

"When once magistrates act contrary to their office, and the end of their institution; when they rob and ruin the public, instead of being guardians of its peace and welfare; they immediately cease to be the ordinance and ministers of God; and no more deserve that glorious character than common pirates and highwaymen.

"Not to discontinue our allegiance, in this case, would be to join with the sovereign in promoting the slavery and misery of that society, the welfare of which, we ourselves, as well as our sovereign, are indispensably obliged to secure and promote, as far as in us lies." [32]

> **Samuel West's** election sermon, "Discourse VI," preached to the Massachusetts Legislature in Boston, Massachusetts, May 29, 1776:

"A slavish submission to tyranny is a proof of a very sordid and base mind. ... all good magistrates, while they faithfully discharge the trust reposed in them, ought to be religiously and conscientiously obeyed. ... The reason why the magistrate is called the minister of God is because he is to protect, encourage, and honor them that do well, and to punish them that do evil; therefore it is our duty to submit to them, not merely for fear of being punished by them, but out of regard to the divine authority, under which they are deputed to execute judgment and to do justice. ... If magistrates have no authority but what they derive from the people; ... if the whole end and design of their institution is to promote the general good, and to secure to men their just rights, it will follow, that when they act contrary to the end and design of their creation they cease being magistrates, and the people which gave them their authority have the right to take it from them again. ... When a people find themselves cruelly

32. Mayhew, Jonathan, 1749–50 multi-discourse sermon, "A Discourse Concerning Unlimited Submission and Non-Resistance to the Higher Powers", Thornton, John Wingate (1860). *The pulpit of the American revolution: Or, The political sermons of the period of 1776 With a historical introduction, notes, and illustrations* (Boston: Gould and Lincoln), pp. 39–104.

oppressed by the parent state, they have an undoubted right to throw off the yoke, and to assert their liberty, ... for, in this case, by the law of self-preservation, which is the first law of nature, they have not only an undoubted right, but it is their indispensable duty, if they cannot be redressed any other way, to renounce all submission to the government that has oppressed them, and set up an independent state of their own. ... No man, therefore, can be a good member of the community that is not as zealous to oppose tyranny as he is ready to obey magistracy. ...

"Further: if magistrates are no farther ministers of God than they promote the good of the community, then obedience to them neither is nor can be unlimited; for it would imply a gross absurdity to assert that, when magistrates are ordained by the people solely for the purpose of being beneficial to the state, they must be obeyed when they are seeking to ruin and destroy it. This would imply that men were bound to act against the great law of self-preservation, and to contribute their assistance to their own ruin and destruction, in order that they may please and gratify the greatest monsters in nature, who are violating the laws of God and destroying the rights of mankind. Unlimited submission and obedience is due to none but God alone. ... Whenever, then, the ruler encourages them that do evil, and is a terror to those that do well, i.e., as soon as he becomes a tyrant, he forfeits his authority to govern, and becomes the minister of Satan, and, as such, ought to be opposed. ... Reason and revelation, we see, do both teach us that our obedience to rulers is not unlimited, but that resistance is not only allowable, but an indispensable duty in the case of intolerable tyranny and oppression." [33]

---

33. West, Samuel, election sermon, "Discourse VI," preached to the Massachusetts Legislature in Boston, Massachusetts, on May 29, 1776, Thornton, John Wingate (1860). *The pulpit of the American revolution: Or, The political sermons of the period of 1776 With a historical introduction, notes, and illustrations* (Boston: Gould and Lincoln), pp 259–322.

Conclusion

In conclusion, both a proper exegesis of Scripture and a careful study of history show that *unlimited* submission to government is unreasonable, unbiblical, and therefore, not required of Christians—or anyone else for that matter. To argue otherwise, as was pointed out earlier, stretches the bounds of credulity.

As we asked earlier, had we been living in the nineteenth century, would we have stood by and done nothing while our neighbors were trapped in slavery? Had we been living in Germany in the 1930s–'40s, would we have submitted to the Nazis and allowed millions of our neighbors to be wrongfully imprisoned and slaughtered without lifting a finger in defiance? Would our excuse have been that Romans 13:1–5 wouldn't allow us to rebel against the government?

If the answers to those and similar questions is a resounding "No," then how can we argue that we must submit to the ungodly, unjust laws and decisions of the Congress and the U.S. Supreme Court today? Are we required by Scripture to submit to a Supreme Court decision like *Roe v. Wade* that has allowed millions of innocent preborn babies to be murdered? How can anyone argue that we should submissively "bide our time" until that *magical moment* when there are enough justices appointed to the Court who will reverse the killing—all while millions continue to be murdered in the meantime? Given the evil of this single Court decision, how can anyone argue that it would be *sinful, illegal* or *anarchistic* to defy it? Instead, it would be the highest act of wickedness not to do so!

I must be clear: this is not an excuse for un-Christian behavior or anarchism. But, it is a call for American Christians to righteously stand up against immoral decrees/laws and do what we can to turn the tide and help establish true justice for all. In states like Oklahoma where I live, there are enough true Christians that if the church shouted with one mighty voice, we could alter the course of our state and possibly start a wave that would sweep through other like-minded states resulting, hopefully, in another great awakening.

In the end, Christians should feel no guilt in refusing to bow in blind servitude to the state or federal government—especially when obeying them requires disobeying God. It is time for Christians in America (where governmental authority resides with *the people*) to decide if we will be governed by the "consent of the governed" or by the "consent of the government." To borrow a few words from the great Christian patriot, Patrick Henry, "I know not what course others may take, but as for me, give me liberty, or give me death!"